Also by Donald N

Twixt Castle and Mart

Best wishes on
your 90th Birthday
from
Mary and Robert

PERTH: AS OTHERS SAW US

Perth:
As Others Saw Us

AN ANTHOLOGY

compiled by

DONALD N. M. PATON

TIPPERMUIR
· BOOKS LIMITED ·

This edition published and copyright 2014 by
Tippermuir Books Limited, Perth, Scotland –
tippermuirbooks@blueyonder.co.uk.

ISBN–10 0956337473

ISBN–13 978–0–9563374–7–4

A CIP catalogue record for this book is available from the British Library.

Illustrations copyright © Rob Hands
Project coordination by Paul Philippou
Book design and artwork by Bernard Chandler, Glastonbury, England
www.graffik.co.uk. Body text set in Bauer Bodoni 11pt on 16pt.
Cover illustration by Rob Hands.

Printed and bound in Great Britain by CPI Antony Rowe, Chippenham and Eastbourne.

To Wilma

By night, by day, a-field, at hame,
The thoughts o thee my breast inflame
And ay I muse and sing thy name –
I only live to love thee.

Robert Burns

'Great Tay, through Perth, through towns,
through country flies,
Perth the whole Kingdom with her
wealth supplies.'

FOREWORD

I first met Donald Paton when he arrived at my office to invite me, as the new Provost, to the prestigious annual dinner of the Perth Burns Club in 2013. We established an easy rapport from the start, assisted by our mutual interest in Scotland's National Bard and the Scots language.

It was Donald that I approached to assist me in establishing a new event in the civic calendar, the Provost's Supper, which would be a celebration of our culture and the unstinting contribution from members of the many diverse and dynamic communities across Perthshire and Kinross-shire. This annual event has enabled me, as Provost, to encourage a more culturally inclusive civic role.

The subject of Donald's new book is a fascinating topic, pulling together various snippets from travellers' journeys over the years to the Fair City of Perth. It must have been a very interesting project for Donald, to scour the many accounts and observations of his home city which encompassed varying writing styles, poetry and journalism going back some hundreds of years. The book really captures the imagination of how Perth would have been and, as Donald has compiled his findings in chronological order, we get a real sense of the social and environmental changes which have occurred over the past five centuries.

Whilst the book was not intended to be a social history of Perth, given the topic it's very difficult for it not to be. Donald has very clearly shown how Perth and its citizens were seen through the eyes of not only visitors, but also local residents. In fact, given Perth's central location in Scotland, it is not surprising that it received its fair share of visitors.

Donald has captured the observations of visitors from the seventeenth, eighteenth and early nineteenth centuries, long before the modern convenience of rail travel. In this modern world, with easy access to our own and public transport, the reader gets a sense of how challenging it would have been to travel even relatively short distances across the country.

At that time, Perth was a major exporter of products such as linen, leather and whisky and with the growing country sports activities, coupled with the introduction of the railway system and the growth of inns and hotels, more people were travelling and Perth found itself becoming a hub of tourist and business activity.

Perth sits on the banks of Scotland's longest river, the Tay, with a rich and influential history that stretches back over 800 years. Perth has served as its country's capital and has always been one of the most important political, judicial and commercial centres in Scotland. Today, with the re-instatement of city status, Perth in the twenty-first century has the opportunity to metamorphose, once again, into a vibrant and dynamic place where people want to live, work and visit.

For all the readers of Donald's latest book, enjoy.

Liz Grant

Provost, Perth & Kinross

ACKNOWLEDGEMENTS

During the course of researching and producing *Perth: As Others Saw Us* I received valued assistance from a variety of sources who embraced the idea with commitment and enthusiasm.

I wish to extend and acknowledge my gratitude to the following owners of copyright, authors, publishers and literary agents who have kindly given permission for poems and passages of prose to appear in this anthology:

Anova Book Group Ltd (London) for the extract from *The Central Highlands* by Ian Finlay, published by Batsford

Birlinn Ltd (Edinburgh) for the Brian Cox article in *A Sense of Belonging to Scotland*

Buckingham Palace for the speech by Her Majesty the Queen at Perth in July 2012

Jeremy Duncan for the extract from his book *Perth: A Century of Change*

Douglas Eadie for his article in *Scottish Field* and his poems which appeared in *Gambit* magazine

The family of the late Duncan Fraser for the extract from *Discovering East Scotland*

The extract from *Highways and Byways in the Central Highlands* by Seton Gordon, published by MacMillan and Company Ltd (London), is reproduced by permission of **James Macdonald Lockhart** Copyright Seton Gordon Literary Estate and Raymond Eagle, FSA Scot., West Vancouver

Robert Hale Ltd (London) for the extract from *Portrait of Perth, Angus and Fife* by David Graham-Campbell

Dr Simon Harding and the Harding family for the extract from
On Flows the Tay by Bill Harding, published by Cualann Press, Dunfermline

Herald & Times Group for permission to reproduce an extract from the
article *Back in Bloom* by Jack Webster, which appeared in *The Herald* on
13 May 1995

The extract from *Fallen Gods* by Quintin Jardine is reproduced by
permission of **Headline Publishing Group (London) and Quintin Jardine**

Maggie Lennon and I. C. S. Books (Glasgow) for the extract from
Small Country: Ten Years of The Scottish Review

Little, Brown Book Group (London) for the extract from *The Steep
Approach to Garbadale* by Iain Banks

Mainstream Publishing (Edinburgh) for the articles by Graham Ogilvy, Ann
Gloag, Geoff Brown and Jean McCormack in *The River Tay and Its People*

McClelland & Stewart (Toronto) for permission to reprint an excerpt from
An Innocent in Scotland: More Curious Rambles and Singular Encounters
by David McFadden. Copyright 1999 David W. McFadden

George MacDiarmid for his song *Perth My Fair City*

Methuen Publishing (London) for the H. V. Morton extract from
In Search Of Scotland

Ian Morton for permission to use the extracts from *The Dusty Road From
Perth* by his late father James Morton, published by Douglas & McIntyre
(Vancouver)

Kenneth Roy for the extracts from *Travels in a Small Country*, published by
Carrick Publishing (Ayr) and for his article in *The Scottish Review*

Michael W. Russell MSP and Neil Wilson Publishing (Glasgow) for the
extract from *In Waiting: Travels in the Shadow of Edwin Muir*

Scotsman Publications (Edinburgh) and Peter Ross for the article from *Scotland on Sunday*

The Spectator (London) for the article by Roy Kerridge

Kenneth Steven for the extract from *Enjoying Scotland* by his late father Campbell Steven, published by Perth & Kinross District Libraries

D. C. Thomson & Company Ltd (Dundee) and Stuart Cosgrove for the article in *The People's Perth* published by *The Courier*

D. C. Thomson & Company Ltd (Dundee) for permission to reprint the article by Colin Gibson from *The Courier's* 'Nature Diary'

Frederick Warne & Company (London) for the extract from *The Journal of Beatrix Potter*

Whilst every effort has been made to identify and contact the copyright owners of works which are not in the public domain, in some cases this has not proved possible. If copyright has unintentionally been infringed then I accept full responsibility and offer my apologies to those concerned.

My grateful thanks go to Provost Liz Grant for so kindly sparing time from her civic duties to write the foreword to this book.

I am most appreciative of the help and facilities extended to me by the staff of the Local Studies department of the A. K. Bell Library, Perth; Steve Connelly, Perth & Kinross Council archivist; Lara Haggarty at the Innerpeffray Library, by Crieff, Perthshire; the National Library of Scotland, Edinburgh; and the Special Collections department at the University of Glasgow.

I would like to acknowledge the role of Paul Philippou and Rob Hands of Tippermuir Books who encouraged, challenged and contained me with their patience, advice and guidance over the course of the project. I particularly valued and appreciated Paul's boundless enthusiasm, perceptiveness, creativity and meticulous attention to detail and design and special thanks go to Rob for producing the inspiring and striking illustrations.

Finally, I thank my wife Wilma for her gentle support and continuous encouragement and for understanding my need of times of solitude to research, compile and write this anthology. This book is dedicated to her with love.

*   *   *

CONTENTS

NINETEENTH CENTURY

TWENTIETH CENTURY

LIST OF ILLUSTRATIONS

DRAWINGS BY ROB HANDS

*   *   *

INTRODUCTION

For many years, one of my minor pleasures has been the reading of old travel journals, diaries, books and articles on Scotland, particularly those relating to my home town of Perth. Such material provides essential information for a social historian.

This book is not intended to be a history of Perth. Many other excellent books have already been written on this subject by historians far more knowledgable than myself. The purpose of this one is to paint a picture of Perth and its people as seen through the eyes of both visitors and residents over a span of five centuries. It is fascinating to read these accounts (not always entirely complimentary) and to consider the social and environmental changes which have occurred with the passage of time. This selection draws on a wide range of prose and poetry, journalism and analysis, from the distant and more recent past. To understand today's Perth, one has to know something of the Perth of yesterday.

In the words of H. V. Morton, 'writers began to explore Scotland soon after the claymore had been sheathed' and Perth's strategic situation in the heart of Scotland meant that it received its fair share of visitors. While some early travellers such as William Cobbett, William Wordsworth, James Johnson, Samuel Johnson and James Boswell appear to have bypassed Perth during their Scottish tours, those who did choose to spend some time in our city have left vivid accounts of their impressions and experiences.

In compiling this anthology, I was fascinated by the writings of the early visitors to Perth, particularly those of the eighteenth and early nineteenth centuries, before the convenience of rail travel. In this modern age, when one can be halfway across the world in a matter of hours, it is interesting to consider how exciting and demanding it must have been for those intrepid travellers of long ago. Until the middle of the nineteenth century, a trip to and around Scotland was a serious undertaking. It took a week to get from London to Edinburgh, and probably even longer in bad weather. Hours spent in the confined interior of a jolting stagecoach, brief stops in the middle of the day to eat, the prospect of uncertain overnight accommodation and the sheer fatigue of the journey meant that our pre-railway travellers required both determination and forbearance. The growth of the Scottish railway system encouraged increasing tourist traffic and this, in turn, led to the growth of inns and hotels. By the 1880s, Perthshire had become widely accessible and the way was opened for the commercial development of the grouse moors and a huge influx of visitors from south of the border.

From the obscurity of library shelves, archives and newspaper files, I have been able to rescue much interesting writing that deserves a wider audience. There are many accounts of Perth, frequently quoted because of the liveliness of style of the various writers, which are now out of print and hard to come by. The purpose of this anthology is to give the reader a flavour of them making them available before they become less and less familiar. Such writing forms a major part of Perth's rich heritage.

I have tried, as far as possible, to keep to chronological order and in most cases I have retained the original spelling and punctuation. Only very occasionally have I made any amendments or discreetly modernised the spelling, where, not to do so, might have resulted in unintelligibility. I have recorded the sources from which virtually all extracts have been taken, and given the writer's dates wherever ascertainable. Brief biographies on most of the writers are listed at the end of the book.

As in any anthology, the selection reflects the compiler's tastes and prejudices. I have included what interested, engaged or amused me and this has brought together some improbable bedfellows! I hope that this book will give pleasure to many and that, in enjoying it, readers may also gain an understanding of the past, present and perhaps the future of this Fair City.

Donald N. M. Paton, FSA Scot.,
Perth, 2014

THE
Seventeenth Century

St John's Kirk

1618   **John Taylor**

FROM STIRLING, I rode to Saint Johnstone, a fine town it is, but it is much decayed, by reason of the want of his Majesty's (James VI) yearly coming to lodge there. There I lodged one night at an inn, the good man of the house his name being Patrick Pitcairne, where my entertainment was with good cheer, good lodging, and too good to a bad weary guest. Mine host told me that the Earl of Mar, and Sir William Murray of Abercairney, were gone to the great hunting at the Brae of Mar. But if I made haste I might perhaps find them at a town called Brekin, or Brechin, 32 miles from St Johnstone.

c.1628   **Henry Adamson**

The Muses Threnodie (An extract)

And there, hard by a river side, they found
The fairest and most pleasant plat of ground
That since by bank of Tiber they had beene,
The like for beauty seldome had they seene
...which when they did espy,
Incontinent they Campus Martius cry,
And as a happie presage they had seene,
They fixt their tents amidst that spacious greene,
Right where now Perth doth stand.

How can I choose, but mourne? When I think on
Our games, Olympick-like, in times agone.
Chiefly wherein our cunning we did try,
And matchless skill in noble archerie.
In these, our days, when archers did abound
In Perth, then famous for such pastimes found:

Among the first, for archers we were known,
And for that art our skill was loudly blown:
What time Perth's credit did stand with the best
And bravest archers this land hath possesst.
We spar'd nor gaines nor paines for to report
To Perth the worship, by such noble sport;
Witness the links of Leith, where Cowper, Grahame,
And Stewart won the prize, and brought it home;
And in these games did offer ten to three
There to contend: Quorum pars magni fui.

1655   Thomas Tucker

ST JOHNSTON, an handsome walled town, with a cittadell added thereunto of late yeares, lying a good way up the river Tay, where there is a wayter (excise man) always attending, not soe much because of any greate tradeing there, as to prevent the carryeing out wools, skyns and hide of which commodities great plenty is brought thither out of the Highlands and there bought and engrossed by the Lowland men.

1685   The Reverend Thomas Morer

A Short Account of Scotland

THERE ARE TWO long spacious streets, besides others of less moment, for intercourse, which being well paved are at all times tolerably clean. The houses are not stately, but after the Scotch way make a good appearance.

Here are only two churches; but one of them so big it looks more like a cathedral than parish church, kept in good repair and decent within. The trade of the town depends chiefly on linen, which the Highlanders bring thither, and which they export to the value of forty thousand pounds sterling per annum... It is a county town governed by a Lord Provost and Bailiffs, has the stile of Royal Borough with the honours and privileges of the most eminent places in Scotland; and the inhabitants speak very big whenever they have occasion to mention the city.

* * *

THE
Eighteenth Century

The House on the Green

1723 John Macky

A Journey Through Scotland in Familiar Letters
from a Gentleman Here to a Friend Abroad

PERTH IS PLEASANTLY SITUATED in a spacious plain,
on the west banks of the River Tay, twenty miles from the sea, and
navigable to this town; it is a compact little town, consisting of two
principal streets from East to West, and several cross lanes from North
to South, the houses so thickly built that it quarter'd with ease Four
Thousand Men, when the Earl of Mar made it his Head Quarters
during the Rebellion; at which time it grew to Rich, by the expence of
the Nobility that flock'd hither on that occasion, and the expence of
the Dutch troops afterwards, that they have built themselves a very
fine Guild Hall, a handsome piece of architecture, and several other
publick and private buildings. The Church of St. John's from whence
it is sometimes called St. John's Town, stands in the middle of the
Town, and is now divided into two neat churches.

Here is a vast trade for Linnen, and it is the Capital of
Perthshire, the largest County in Scotland. Here is an old Palace, which
devolv'd to the Crown by the Conspiracy of the Gowry's, a story that
hath made so good a noise all over Europe.

1724–7 Daniel Defoe

A Tour Thro' the Whole Island of Great Britain

THE RIVER TAY is, without exception, the greatest river
in Scotland, and of the longest course, for it rises out of the mountains,
on the edge of Argyle Shire; and running first north into the shire of
Bradalbin, there receiving many other rivers, it spreads itself into a
large lake, which is called Lough Tay, extending for forty miles in
length, and traversing the very heart of Scotland, comes into the sea

near this place: Now, as I design to keep in this part of my work to the east coast of the country, I must for the present quit the Tay itself, keeping a little on the hither side of it, and go back to that part of the country which lies to the south, and yet east of Dunbarton and Lenox shires; so drawing an imaginary line from Stirling Bridge, due north, through the heart of the country to Inverness, which I take to lye almost due north and south.

In this course then I moved to Perth, lying upon the same River Tay, but on the hither bank. It was formerly called St. Johnston, or St. Johns Town, from an old church, dedicated to the evangelist, St. John, part of which is still remaining, and is yet big enough to make two parochial churches, and serve the whole town for their public worship.

The chief business of this town is the linnen manufacture; and it is so considerable here, all the neighbouring country being employed in it, that it is a wealth to the whole place. The Tay is navigable up to the town for ships of good burthen: and they ship off here so great a quantity of linnen, (all for England) that all the rest of Scotland is said not to ship off so much more.

This town was unhappily for some time, the seat of the late Rebellion; but I cannot say it was unhappy for the Town: For the townsmen got so much money by both parties, that they are evidently enriched by it; and it appears not only by the particular families and persons in the town, but by their publick and private buildings which they have rais'd since that; as particularly a new Tolbooth or Town-Hall.

The salmon taken here, and all over the Tay, is extremely good, and the quantity prodigious. They carry it to Edinburgh, and to all the towns where they have no salmon, and they barrel up a great quantity for exportation: The merchants of this town have also a considerable trade to the Baltick, to Norway, and especially, since as above, they were enriched by the late Rebellion.

It seems a little enigmatic to us in the South, how a rebellion should enrich any place;

But a few words will explain it. First, I must premise, that the Pretender and his troops lay near, or in this place a considerable time; now the bare consumption of victuals and drink, is a very considerable advantage in Scotland, and therefore 'tis frequent in Scotland for towns to petition the government to have regiments of soldiers quartered upon them, which in England would look monstrous, nothing being more terrible and uneasy to our towns in England.

Again, as the Pretender and his troops lay in the neighbourhood, namely at Scoone, so a very great confluence of the nobility, clergy, and gentry, however fatally, as to themselves, gathered about him, and appeared here also; making their court to him in person, and waiting the issue of his fortunes, till they found the storm gathering from the south, and no probable means to resist it, all relief from abroad being every where disappointed, and then they shifted off as they could.

While they resided here, their expense of money was exceeding great; lodgings in the town of Perth let for such a rate, as was never known in the place before; trade was in a kind of hurry, provision dear: In a word, the people, not of the town only, but of all the country round, were enriched; and had it lasted two or three months longer, it would have made all the towns rich.

When this cloud was dispersed, and all the party fled and gone, the victors entered, the general officers and the loyal gentlemen succeeded the abdicated and routed party; but here was still the head quarters, and afterwards the Dutch troops continued here most part of the winter; all this while the money flowed in, and the town made their market on both sides; for they gained, by the Royal Army's being on that side of the country, and by the foreigners being quartered there, almost as much, tho' not in so little time as by the other.

The town was well built before, but now has almost a new

face; (or as I said) here are abundance of new houses, and more old houses new fitted and repaired, which look like new. The linen trade too, which is their main business, has mightily increased since the Act of Parliament in England, for the suppressing the use and wearing of printed calicoes; so that the manufacture is greatly increased here, especially of that kind of cloth which they buy here and send to England to be printed, and which is so much used in England in the room of the calicoes, that the worsted and silk weavers in London seem to have very little benefit by the Bill, but that the linnen of Scotland and Ireland are, as it were, constituted in the room of the calicoes.

1749   Major-General James Peter Wolfe

Instructions to Young Officers

PERTH. OCT. 27, 1749 – All the detachments are to report to the commanding officer at Perth once a fortnight, and with their first report they are to send a copy of their orders they receive from the commissioned and non-commissioned officers they relieve. It is to be a standing order in the regiment, that when pay is ordered for parties, the money is to be given to the officer that commands. Watchcoats are to be delivered to the serjeant of the guard for all sentries; they are to be worn from the retreat to troop-beating in the morning only.

NOV. 10 – The officers are desired to observe the orders that have been given for frequently visiting the soldiers quarters, that they may be informed of their behaviour, and know in what manner they diet, and if the quarters are kept clean.

The serjeants and corporals are to give in an account in writing to the commanding officers of companies of the manner in which the different squads mess, the number that eats together, the houses where they diet, whether in their quarters or out, specifying the persons names that entertain such soldiers as do not eat in their quarters.

If any woman in the regiment has a venereal disorder, and does not immediately make it known to the surgeon, she shall upon the first discovery be drummed out of the regiment, and be imprisoned in the Tolbooth if ever she returns to the corps.

The major observes, that the worst and idlest soldiers are those that are most frequently in venereal disorders, by which they are incapable of serving, and their duty is done by better men; he therefore thinks they should suffer for their intemperance; and orders that 6 s. be paid for the cure of the pox, and 4s. for the clap; which sum of money to be employed in providing necessaries and conveniences for the hospital; and when the man cured, the money is immediately to be paid him by the company in order to its being laid out for the common benefit of sick soldiers.

JAN. 1, 1750 – The soldiers may understand from the severity of the punishment from last Monday and today, that a want of honesty and fidelity will be attended with the worst consequences to themselves, and that whoever acts the part of a villain must expect all the rigour of the strictest justice.

A list to be given tomorrow at orderly time of the number of women in the regiment that sell liquor of any kind, and the streets they live in, and by whose permission it is that they sell such liquors, that proper measures may be taken to prevent their contributing to the uncommon villainies that have brought a reproach upon the regiment.

MAY 30 – The shameful drunkenness observed among the men, on pay-days in particular, is thought in a great measure to proceed from their not putting in a proportion of their pay regularly into their messes: the officers are to remember they have been more than once required to consider that any neglect on their part brings the men to disorders and crimes, and consequently to punishment, which would be avoided by a proper care of them, and watch upon their conduct.

It has been observed that the soldiers have of late been employed in all sorts of dirty work, such as carrying coals, filth, &c. in the streets, and have been busy in the holds of several ships: they likewise have condescended to clean the kennels: the colonel is ashamed and surprised to perceive that they are not below the meanest piece of drudgery for the meanest consideration: and since it is plain that they have forgot what character they are in, the colonel for their credit, and the credit of the regiment, absolutely forbids all kind of dirty work whatsoever, and he will punish any offender with severity.

1760   **Bishop Richard Pococke**

Tour of Scotland

WE CAME TO PERTH by the finest turnpike road in Britain, which leads from Edinburgh... This place is most delightfully situated in a most beautiful country, there are small hills to the south and west, the fine river Tay and the rising ground beyond it to the east. It is open to the north on which side is adorned with noble plantations, among which are those of Bussy, belong to Lord Kinnoul, a furlong from the town, and what adds greatly to the picture the waters of the Almond, two miles distant is brought round the town: and in summer is entirely carried off this way. At each end of the town is a large green belonging to the community, which is let to the town at so much a head for cattle; and the north green is much used for bleaching and washing. The town consists chiefly of two streets, from east to west, near half a measured mile long, and two streets which extend to the south, and the other to the north from the great street.

Soon after I arrived the Provost and another of the

Corporation came to see me and with great politeness showed me everything about the town, and in the evening presented me with the freedom of the place.

1769,1772 **Thomas Pennant**

First and Second Tours of Scotland

ASCENDED THE HILL of Moncrief; the prospect from thence is the glory of Scotland, and well merits the eulogia given it for the variety and richness of its views.

To the North lies the town of Perth, with a view of part of its magnificent bridge; which with the fine woods called Perth Parks, the vast plain of Strath–Tay, the winding of that noble river, its islands and the grand boundary formed by the distant Highlands, finish this matchless scene. The inhabitants of Perth are far from being blind to the beauties of their river; for with singular pleasure they relate the tradition of the Roman army, when it came in sight of the Tay, bursting into the exclamation of *Ecce Tiberim*.

On approaching the town are some pretty walks handsomely planted, and at a small distance, the remains of some works of Cromwell's called Oliver's Mount.

Perth is large, well built, and populous, and contains about eleven thousand inhabitants, nine thousand of whom are of the established church of Scotland; the rest of a variety of persuasions, such as Episcopalians, Non-jurors, Glassites, and Seceders. The second chiefly consists of a congregation of venerable females. The town has but one parish, supplied with three churches, besides the chapels for such who dissent from the established church.

The two principal streets are remarkably fine: in some of the lesser are yet a few wooden houses in the old style; but as they decay the magistrates prohibit the rebuilding of them in the old way.

The flourishing state of Perth is owing to two accidents; the first that of Cromwell's wounded officers and soldiers choosing to reside here after he left the Kingdom, who introduced a spirit of industry among the people. The other cause was the long continuance of the Earl of Mar's army here in 1715, which occasioned vast sums of money being spent in the place. But this town as well as all Scotland dates its prosperity from the year 1745; the government of this part of Great Britain never having been settled till a little after that time. The rebellion was a disaster, violent in its operation, but salutary in its effects.

Cross the Tay on a temporary bridge; the stone bridge, which is to consist of nine arches, being at this time unfinished: the largest arch is seventy-six feet wide; when complete, it promises to be a most magnificent structure. The river here is very violent, and admits of scarce any navigation above; but ships one hundred and twenty tons burden come as high as the town; and if flat-bottomed, of even two hundred tons.

The trade of Perth is considerable. Of white and brown linens, about seventy five thousand pounds worth are annually sent to London, besides a very great quantity that is disposed of to Edinburgh and Glasgow. London, Manchester and Glasgow take about ten thousand pounds worth of linen yarn. It exports annually from twenty four to thirty thousand bolls of wheat and barley to London and Edinburgh. The export of cured salmon to London and the Mediterranean brings in from twelve to fourteen thousand pounds annually. That fish is taken here in vast abundance; three thousand have been caught in one morning.

There has been in these parts a very great fishery of pearl, got out of the fresh-water mussels. From the year 1761 to 1764 ten thousand pounds worth were sent to London and sold from ten shillings to one pound sixteen shillings per ounce. I have been told that a pearl has been taken there that weighed thirty three grains. But this fishery is at present exhausted, from the avarice of the undertakers.

1787   **Robert Burns**

From the Journal of his Tour in the Highlands

(FRIDAY, 14 SEPTEMBER) – come thro' the rich harvests and fine hedge rows of the carse of Gowrie, along the romantic margin of the Grampian Hills, to Perth – Castle Huntly – Sir Stewart Threipland.

(SATURDAY, 15 SEPTEMBER) – Perth – Scoon – picture of the Chevalier and his sister – Queen Mary's bed, the hangings wrought with her own hands – fine, fruitful hilly, woody country round Perth – Tay bridge – Mr and Mrs Hastings – Major Scott – Castle Gowrie – leave Perth. Saturday morn – come up Strathearn to Endermay to dine – fine, fruitful cultivated Strath – the scene of 'Bessy Bell and Mary Gray' near Perth – fine scenery on the banks of the May – Mrs Belches, gawcie, frank, affable, fond of rural sports, hunting, &c, – Miss Stirling her sister, *en verite* – come to Kinross to lie – Reflections in a fit of the Colic.

1788   **Elizabeth Diggle**

From her Journal of a Tour from London to the Highlands of Scotland. 19 April to 7 August 1788

ON TUESDAY LAST we went to the ancient palace of Scone which belongs at present to Lord Stormont, & has not much appearance of ancient grandeur about it, but is fitting up in a very comfortable manner for a country house. The church or chapel where the Kings of Scotland used to be crowned is entirely gone, the person who shewed the house far from pointing out any vestige of it could not tell us where it had been. But they shewed us in the house more needle work wrought by Queen Mary's own hands during her confinement at Loch Leven than I think she could have done in her whole life, at least I have certainly seen so much in Scotland. This at Scone was a bed, chairs and tapestry the latter in fine tent stitch some scripture history. The next day we went to Castle Duplin, it is a delightful ride from Perth & the park is beautiful, so that we did not entirely lose our time tho' we could not gain admittance to the house the family being there. Here is a great deal of linen manufactured in the neighbourhood of Perth two large bleaching greens called the Inches one on each side of the town are generally covered in the whitening season, they are prettily planted with trees, & make an agreeable promenade for the inhabitants.

1791   **William Thomas Newte**

Prospects and Observations on a Tour of England
and Scotland – Natural, Economical and Literary

THERE IS NOT ANY TOWN in Scotland that admits of greater improvement than Perth, or that would be more highly improved if it were possessed by inhabitants like those of Glasgow and Aberdeen. Quays would be extended downward on both sides of the Tay: the South Inch, with the new adjacent land to the westward, would be laid out in new streets and squares, according to increasing commerce and population: canals would be formed for conveying the merchandise of the place to the very doors of the shop-keepers, and, in the natural progress of things, as far as possible, into the country. But, however favourably situated for manufactures and trade, it is but of late that a spirit of commercial spirit has visited Perth.

The austere spirit of the Town of Perth, which withstood, for centuries, the influence of many visitors and travellers, and particularly of a large proportion of the soldiery constantly stationed there, begins now, we were informed, in some small measure to relax, as appears from some pleasant stories that are frequent in the mouths of the tradesmen, concerning some of the Ministers thereabouts, as well as the Elders, a species of lay brethren in the church of Scotland, corresponding to the Mahomedan Maraboots, who are raised to a degree of clerical dignity on account of their supposed sanctity, without any previous education. Every parish is divided into a certain number of districts, from four generally to ten, called commonly quarters, in each of which an Elder is appointed for the purpose of visiting and praying.

1792 **John Lettice**

Letters on a Tour Through Various Parts of Scotland

WE ENTERED THE TOWN by an elegant new bridge of nine arches; over which it was impossible to pass, without flopping to contemplate, towards the right side, villas, gardens, and lofty rocks, all beautifully covered with wood on one shore, reflected in the water; the bright green meadows in sweet succession on the opposite side, with the Highland hills and mountains, rising one behind another, and closing the distance in the clouds. These objects, with the shipping on the river, in its various movements, or positions of business, and two streets of the town opening handsomely at angles in front of the bridge, formed altogether, under a bright autumnal day, no unworthy accompaniments of the delightful scenery first described. The left hand street from the bridge introduces the traveller very advantageously into the lower part of the town. It runs a very comfortable length on the strand of the Tay. At right angles to this street, and opening finely into it, are two others of noble breadth, and each near half a mile long. The first of these is the principal street of Perth, and is full of lofty well-built houses; and its perspective, when seen at the bottom of which we first entered, is particularly striking, and of grand effect. This is occupied by the chief inhabitants; the merchants and manufacturers of the place. The other great street running parallel, has little to commend, but that it is wide and rectilinear; the houses being irregularly built, and, in general, mean. The place altogether is large and populous: one part of its inhabitants is employed in the manufacture of linen to a great extent: another in exporting corn, particularly wheat and barley, of which they send great supplies to Edinburgh: a third, in the fishing and curing of salmon, which they export in vast quantities, every season, to the London markets, and to those of their own capital.

From anything in the externals of the town of Perth, we were not led to suppose, that refinement of taste, or luxury in the modes of living or dress, has yet made any remarkable progress among its wealthier inhabitants. Whatever of this nature offered itself to our view, it was in the article of buildings: in which the opulence of most, perhaps of all the towns in North Britain, begins first to show itself to the world. As convenience is generally found to keep pace with elegance in the improvements of architecture, and as few of the refinements of society have duration, more to recommend them, than those of building, the disposition of the Scots, to display their taste in this way, is among the proofs of that grand sense, which I have had frequent opportunity of considering as characteristic of this people. I cannot help mentioning here, that in a walk which we took to review the bridge, we observed an instance in which economy appears to have held too strict rule over taste. This elegant structure has been allowed somewhat less width than conveniently might have been given to it. In consequence of this defect, one side of it only has been paved for foot passengers; nor is it lighted in both. These latter circumstances have a one-ear'd sort of effect, little to the credit of the bridge, and such as its general character has by no means deserved.

Perth, like all other great towns in North Britain, has its public subscription coffee-house, for the perusal of the periodical public prints; and the study of politics may be reckoned one of the favourite amusements of every order of persons in the town.

All the newspapers which we saw there were those least calculated to advance the spirit of optimism, and not all to exercise impartiality of judgement. This one could not but lament. Whether, therefore, the coffee-house contributes very liberally to the good humour, or political candour of the inhabitants, must be left for those to determine, who have more acquaintance with them.

If papers of the same tendency should occupy the chimney-corner of every public-house, I should be inclined to guess, that the bilious and discontented humour of sedentary manufacturers would be more improved by a brisk dance, once or twice a week, to the bagpipe, than by hanging their heads, during their hours of leisure, over the morbid vapours of some factious chronicler.

1792 Robert Heron

Observations made in a Journey through the Western Counties of Scotland

PERTH had been a scene of festivity, since I been last in it. The annual races had been celebrated: and balls and carousals had accompanied the races. Some rising riots had been easily quieted by the prudence of the magistrates, and of the gentlemen whose presence seemed to provoke them. - and, it is fair to add. - through the good temper and good sense of the People in general. The festivities of the occasion went on, uninterrupted; and had been terminated in general harmony among all who had assisted in them.

1796 The Hon. Mrs Sarah Murray of Kensington

A Companion and Useful Guide to the Beauties of Scotland

PERTH is a very ancient town; but within these few years it has been increased to a great degree, so that it may be called a new town.

Its bridge over the Tay, and its two Inches, ornament it wonderfully. The Inches are large flat grass fields, one at the south entrance of Perth, the other at the north; and the roads and walks in them are through avenues of trees. There is a view of the town of Perth coming from the south, where the Romans halted to admire, and cried out with one voice – 'Ecce Tiberim!' I think they paid a very bad compliment to the Tay, as there can be no comparison between it and the sluggish Tiber.

The ground around Perth, I was told, lets from two to three and five pounds a Scotch acre, which is about one-fourth more than an English acre. Butter is about ten-pence a pound, twenty-two ounces. Not only butter, but eggs, and poultry of all sorts are greatly increased in price since the small farms have decreased in number.

As no coal pits have been worked north of the Eckles, or Oichill Hills, that necessary article is brought by water to Perth; the Tay being navigable for considerable vessels as high as that town: and as many, if not more, of the Newcastle coals are burnt there, than of Scotch coals; because they are procured full as cheap, if not more so, than the coals from Fife and Stirlingshire.

The labourer at Perth, gets commonly fifteen-pence a day; in harvest, sixteen-pence, with meat and drink. Masons' wages, twenty-pence a day; their labourers, fourteen-pence.

In the worst street in Perth, part of the old Castle of Gowrie is still remaining; some military men were quartered in it when I was there: notwithstanding, there are very fine barracks erected at the west end of the town. In the Castle of Gowrie, James the First of England was captured by the nobles of that name; from whom he was rescued by the wonderful courage of a very few friends whom had come to Perth with him, and regained his palace in Fifeshire.

Near Perth are a great number of extensive fine bleaching grounds. The chief manufacture of the town are cottons, and the printing of them; also great quantities of men's shoes and boots are made at Perth, and sent to the London market.

The following is the legend of the name of Kinnoull Hill. – Formerly the old town of Perth was situated near the junction of the river Almond with the Tay; and it was washed away by a violent flood. The king's infant son, in his cradle, was hurried down the rushing Tay, in sight of the unhappy father who, distracted, ran along the bank; and when he came to a spot about half a mile above the present town, he made an exclamation in Galic, something like Aicha! from which the east bank took the name of Kincarrica. The king still followed his floating darling; and when he came opposite to the high hill, and the dangerous sweep of the river, below the site of new Perth, his frantic grief and fright made him howl. From that, says the legend, came the name of the Hill of Kinnoull.

1799   Barthélemy Faujas de Saint-Fond

Travels in England, Scotland and the Hebrides

WE REACHED PERTH a little late in the evening, by a road extremely rugged and fatiguing.

The small city of Perth stands in a very agreeable situation on the river Tay, which the tide enters to a considerable distance and renders navigable for small vessels. It is in a pretty flourishing condition, and contains a population of about twelve thousand souls. The stone bridge over the Tay was constructed by the same person who built that of Blackfriars, at London. It is very well executed, but is rather narrow for its length.

Before the reformation took place in England and Scotland, the town of Perth, where the catholic worship reigned in all its splendour, contained some fine religious foundations, besides a number of churches. Of these, the greater part have since been laid in ruins, or converted into churches for the use of the presbyterians. In several of the streets are seen some fine gothic facades, which belonged to cathedrals, chapter-houses, monasteries, and nunneries. These remains of monuments, consecrated to a worship which formerly flourished so vigorously in the three kingdoms, announce that religions, as well as governments, have their periods of instability and revolution, which incessantly succeed each other at intervals of longer or shorter extent, but which, when the impulse is once given, no human power is able to arrest: so true is it, that in morals, as well as in physics, there is nothing durable in this world.

Machines for carding and spinning cotton, had been introduced at Perth only a little before our arrival there. We saw the first of them at the manufactory of an individual who had caused them to be constructed at Manchester. He found it impossible, however, to convey them out of that town but during the night: so jealous are the manufacturers of Manchester of this happy invention of Arkwright, which has given such extensive celebrity and immense advantages to its commerce.

The most considerable manufactures of Perth are fine linen, thread, and flax; and some very excellent articles are produced in this line. Here I saw a loom for weaving very large bed sheets, in one piece, by means of a shuttle fixed on small rollers. A pair of these sheets, made of very fine linen, costs from a hundred and fifty to a hundred and sixty livres of French money. I purchased at a table-cloth manufactory a dozen small napkins and a breakfast-cloth. They were of an excellent quality, and cost me four Louis-d'or. I was happy to have an opportunity of carrying them to France by way of models.

The desire of examining the hill of Kinnoul was what principally determined me to pass through Perth, from which it was only two miles and a quarter distant. I was therefore able to make several visits to it during the three days that I stayed at Perth. The lavas and agates which I collected there were very numerous.

Scarcely had I crossed the bridge of Perth, where I observed some lavas in strata, unformed masses, and ill-shaped prisms. These different currents proceeded from several eminences forming part of the mountain of Kinnoul, the basis of which, occupied a very considerable extent. Pursuing the road along the Tay, with the mountain on my left, for two miles and a quarter, I came to a steep and almost perpendicular rock, nearly six hundred feet high, and on the very edge of the road. The traveller ought to make directly for this place, because it is the richest in agates and other productions worth collecting.

1799 **Rowland Hill**

Journal of a Tour through the North of England and Parts of Scotland with Remarks on the Present State of the Established Church of Scotland

THURSDAY MORNING, AUGUST 9. Gave an exhortation to a few people that collected at Inver, near Dunkeld, and proceeded to Perth. Here I preached to a full congregation in the Relief Chapel. The opening of this place of worship was an act of the greatest kindness, as the weather would not have permitted preaching out of doors. Preached from 2 Cor. iii.18. on the glory of God manifested in the glorious Gospel.

c.1799 **Carolina Oliphant**

Kitty Reid's House

Hech! hey! the mirth that was there,
The mirth that was there,
The mirth that was there;
Hech! how! the mirth that was there,
In Kitty Reid's house on the green, jo.

There was laughin' and singin', an' dancin' and glee
In Kitty Reid's house, in Kitty Reid's house,
There was laughin' and singin', an' dancin' and glee,
In Kitty Reid's house on the green, jo.

Hech! hey! the fright that was there,
The fright that was there,
The fright that was there;
Hech! how! the fright that was there,
In Kitty Reid's house on the green, jo.
The light glimmer'd in thro' a crack i' the wa',
An' a'body thought the lift it would fa',
An' lads and lasses they sune ran awa'
Frae Kitty Reid's house on the green, jo.

Hech! hey! the dule that was there,
The dule that was there,
The dule that was there;
The birds an' beasts it wauken'd them a',
In Kitty Reid's house on the green, jo.
The wa' gaed a hurly an' scatter'd them a',
The piper, the fiddler, an' Kitty, an a',
The kye fell a routin', the cocks they did craw,
In Kitty Reid's house on the green, jo.

(Another older version of the song mentions the names of some who frequented the house.)

Kirkpottie, Kintullo, Pitcur an' Lord Rollo,
Cam' a' to this house, to Kitty Reid's house;
Invermay, Monivaird, Balbeggie, Kinnaird,
Cam' a' to the house on the green, jo.

Gan' tell Tullylum that he's wanted to come
To Kitty Reid's house, to Kitty Reid's house;
Tell Bousie an' Kerr, and Ruthven the peer,
To come to the house on the green, jo.

(The House on the Green was a famous Perth hostelry which was formerly the town home of the Mercer family. It was situated at the corner of High Street and Watergate near The Cross of Perth. The hostess was Kitty Reid and the establishment was much favoured by the county lairds.)

* * *

THE

Nineteenth Century

South Inch and Walter Scott statue

1800   **Dr John Leyden**

Journal of a Tour in the Highlands and Western Islands
of Scotland in 1800

FROM ST MARTINS we proceeded to Perth along the
Aberdeen road. The view of Perth as we descended upon the town is
extremely beautiful. The declivities were covered with corn-fields and
trees, and the green hills which surmount it on the north and south,
especially that of Moncrieff, are soft and romantic, displaying many
elegant mansions in their recesses. As you approach, the buildings are
extremely good, and the plan of the town is very regular. Tay bridge
is a noble object, and the views up and down the river are sweet and
picturesque. The ruin of Castle Gowrie is in no respect remarkable,
except for having been the scene of one of those obscure facts in history
which afford a wide range for conjecture, but defy elucidation.

I left Perth in that pleasant and amusing state of mind which
is something between regret and chagrin, and does not appear to have
been accurately described by philosophers. Whether it was the motion
of the post-chaise, which gives a cheerful circulation to the fluids;
whether it was the succession of new scenes or the succession of my
own thoughts, I shall not pretend to determine; but I found by the time
that we had gained the summit of Moncrieff Hill I had regained my
usual serenity. Here we paused to enjoy the view, which is delightful;
and it was here it was that the Romans, advancing against our
invincible ancestors, paused in astonishment, and, beholding the
majestic Tay, imagined that they had discovered another Tiber. The
range of the Grampian mountains bounds the horizon towards the
north, and the fertile vale of Strathmore occupies the intermediate
space, through which you trace the course of the Tay till your eye is
arrested by the town of Perth, its spires and majestic bridge. The
Kinnoul Crags, emerging boldly towards the river through the woods
which skirt their houses and surround the romantic Kinfauns, are

extremely grand and picturesque. Towards the east expand the rich and fertile Carse of Gowrie and the Firth of Tay. The view towards the south extends over the fertile and cultivated district of Strathearn, which has not the variety of the Strath of Tay, though it resembles it in softness and beauty. The Earn is a majestic river, but its banks are low, and here not well sheltered with wood. Following the windings, the eye passes over Abernethy and rest upon the green range of the Lomond Hills. After passing the Brig of Earn, we left the Highlands behind us with regret and ascended the range of the Ochil Hills, from which we had another fine view of Strathearn.

1802   **Alexander Campbell**

A Journey from Edinburgh through Parts of North Britain

IT HAS BEEN ASSERTED, that Perth benefited much by the circulation of money in the rebellions of 1715 and 1745, owing to its central situation as a military post; and, that many invalids of Cromwell's army, in 1654, remaining by choice in and near Perth, set an example of activity and industry of utmost importance to the natives. Hence arose the spirit for speculation and enterprise to manifest at this day.

In our retrospective of the rise and progress of the trade and commerce of Perth, we find that, towards the middle of the seventeenth century, it was a place of considerable importance.

The principal taverns, hotels, and coffee houses in Perth are regularly supplied with the London and provincial news-papers and literary journals. The fine arts advance apace. Print-shops, music-shops, and booksellers-shops, appear in almost every street. Of the latter, many carry on trade to a considerable extent; and not a few keep circulating libraries.

These improvements are highly characteristic of the times; and the inhabitants of Perth are rapidly on the advance in refinement of manners and the elegant blandishments of fashionable society. It may afford matter of curious information to exhibit a trait of the inhabitants of this city two hundred years ago, in contrast with the manners of those of the present day. Soon after the Reformation, when profane dramas were publicly represented, it appears from a record, dated June 3rd, 1589, that there were a company of comedians then at Perth, who found it necessary to apply to the consistory for a licence to perform plays; as an act of Assembly had passed in the year 1574–5, prohibiting the people, under pain of church censure, from resorting to such profane exhibitions. The words of the record are as follows: *'Perth, June 3rd, 1589. The ministers and elders give licence to plai the plai, with conditions that no swearing, banning, nor onie feurility sall be spoken, which would be a scandal to our religion which we profess, and for an evil example unto others. Alswa that nothing sall be added to what is the register of the plai itself. If anyone who plais sal do in the contrarie, he sal make his public repentance (i.e. be imprisoned, and afterwards appear in church, to be rebuked in the public place of repentance.),* The clergy of the present day, who still view the stage through optics that greatly magnify the danger arising from its immoral tendency, are less rigid in their conduct towards it; and players occasionally, in their peregrinations through the north, remain in Perth for a considerable length of time; a proof of their being kindly entertained, encouraged, and rewarded.

It is said, 'that the manners of the people, till long after the reformation of religion, were exceedingly licentious' in Perth. Church-discipline, however, seems to have checked that degree of unrestrained, indulgence, imbibed, no doubt, by the laity from the evil example which the clergy of the religious houses, formerly so numerous in that city, exhibited in their dissolute and hypocritical lives. 'Now I see that God's judgements are just', said an aged matron when beholding the palace and abbey of Scone on fire, (27th June, 1599) 'and that no man is able to save, where he will punish. This place, since I remember, hath been nothing but a den of whoremongers: it is incredible how many wives have been adulterated.'

1803 **The Reverend James Hall**

Travels in Scotland by an Unusual Route

REPAIRING TO MY ALE-HOUSE, at Road-End, I remounted my pony, and came slowly to Perth; which, with its fine environs, has also often been described. The river rolling in great majesty between the cliff of Kinnoull and the hill of Moncrieff; the island formed by the disjunction of the river into two parts a little below Perth, these now exulting in their reunion; the South Inch; an extensive and beautiful lawn, bounded on the east by the Tay, on the north by the town and suburbs, and fringed all round with a waving avenue of trees – these objects, as you approach Perth, would slacken the course of the most insensible traveller.

It is well-known that Perth, with Scone, almost contiguous, was considered as the capital of Scotland even so far down as the middle of the fifteenth century. Whoever glances at its situation on the map, scarcely needs to be told of the number of national and ecclesiastical councils that have been held here; the armies lodged in or encamped near it, the sieges it underwent, and the battles fought in its vicinity. It recalls to the mind very many of the most important passages in the history of Scotland.

I have been informed by a person, who, having been educated at Perth school, and resided long very near it, that the Perthians were, about forty years ago, distinguished by a high degree of conceit and arrogance, claiming great consideration as the citizens of what was so long, and still ought to be, the first city in Scotland. They inherited, by tradition, somewhat of that self-confidence and presumption, which are wont to belong to the natives of places that are the seat of government. And to this, perhaps, he thinks we are indebted for the boldness with which they took the lead in the reformation. Whatever may be thought of this refinement, we certainly recognize in Perth, and the provincial parishes, very much of the *fervidum gentus scotorum*, from the time when they smashed the images in the churches, and the women reviled, beat, and put to flight the priests, to the present.

As to the lower classes, I mean the poorer, when they went to one anothers' houses, the guest, in return for the victuals, was at the expense of the drink – ale or whisky, for which they sent to the public-house. A genteeler and more hospitable turn now prevails among not a few of the opulent citizens of Perth; and will no doubt make its way, in some degree, among the whole. But, as yet, Perth cannot be called a polite or a hospitable place.

The town is thriving in trade and manufactures; and, from the circumstances, arising from its situation, of having no rival town for twenty miles or more distant, has many advantages in the retail trade, by which many of its people live in opulence. The town of Perth is extending to the north, south and west. In this last direction it has begun to stretch even beyond the Royalty. Its present population is twenty thousand souls. Its exports are, linen cloth of all kinds, cotton stuffs, salmon, grain, shoes, and, perhaps, some other articles of less value. It imports all that the country wants, but does not produce. The chief trade of Perth is with London and the Baltic. The salmon fishery of the Tay connects it in some measure too with the Mediterranean.

While I was at Perth, it was impossible not to take a walk up the Tay to Scone. The vestiges of the pavement, and bridges over every rivulet and rill on the road thither, have an air of antiquity that accords well with the expectation of seeing the ancient palace of the kings of Scotland.

c.1807 **Peter Agnew**

Sweet Perth

Sweet Perth is the glory and pride of the nation
She's envied by her neighbours, but what can they say?
She's pleasantly placed in a fine situation,
And O! She looks meek on the banks of the Tay.

To honour my native, 'tis surely my duty,
I'll sing of the city in which I was born.
For fine architecture, compactness and beauty,
Now Bertha may laugh all her sisters to scorn.

Some say Agricola the city first founded;
And O, he was glad when he saw such a plain,
With hills and with valleys so neatly surrounded,
And where she now stands he encamped his men.

Serene from tornados and swells of the ocean,
Like Mars-field, like Rome, and like Tiber they cried.
Refreshed in Eden, and cherished in Goshen,
To buildings and fencings their hands they applied.

1807 **Sir John Carr**

Caledonian Sketches or A Tour Through
Scotland in 1807

WITH AN EXCEPTION of the New Town, Edinburgh, the
town of Perth, the capital of the county of Perthshire, is by far the best
built and most regular of any in Scotland. Perhaps a finer situation for

a capital could not be found. The streets are broad and long, well paved, with handsome buildings on either side, and many elegant shops. It appears that anciently particular streets were inhabited by particular artisans, as the names of some still preserved, seem to indicate. The inns are excellent. It would be tedious and foreign to my purpose to describe this beautiful city very minutely; it will be sufficient to observe that the principal streets, in the old part of the town, are the High and the South street, both of which are very long, and that George-street, Charlotte-street, the Crescent, Rose Terrace, and the Circus, are the most handsome in the new part. This town has been subject to some very destructive inundations, which have caused the streets to be raised from time to time. Many stories, and even whole houses, are to be found below the surface of the street.

The Crescent forms a beautiful curve, and looks towards the North Inch, a lawn of the greenest pasture, forming the Race-Course, and watered by the Tay. This spot is frequently embellished with many elegant and well-dressed ladies, and at the same time disfigured by the linen-washerwomen. On the Rose Terrace, to the northward of the Crescent, stands an elegant building, which was nearly finished, containing the halls and apartments of the public seminaries. This highly ornamental building has been erected by subscription, many of the donations of which are truly noble. The schools of this city have long been very justly celebrated, and have afforded education to many distinguished persons, amongst whom the people of Perth, with infinite pride, reckon James Crichton, whose wonderful endowments, both of body and mind, obtained him the appellation of 'the admirable Crichton', and ranked him as the wonder of his species, and the eloquent, learned and refined Lord Mansfield, who, after obtaining at the British bar, by the invincible powers of his oratory, the name of 'the silver-tongued Murray', filled the dignified office of Chief Justice with a splendour of ability that will shed lustre upon his country for ages to come. The pupils of these seminaries are very numerous, and come from various parts of Great Britain and Ireland.

Much of the prosperity and opulence of Perth are traceable to those causes which seldom produce anything but desolation and poverty. In those unhappy times of public broil, which so frequently occur in Scottish history, this town was occasionally occupied by opposing armies, which rendered it a market for every necessary commodity. Dealers created capitals, and, by their prudence and enterprise, laid the foundation of all the good fortune which has attended this city since the Union.

The prevailing religion is High Calvinism, and the places of worship are numerous. The inhabitants have a high character for sobriety and decorum of manners.

Owing to the number of people of rank and respectability, in commerce and trade, in the city and its vicinity, the streets are frequently enlivened with eloquent equipages. The style of living is very handsome, and the ladies dress with considerable taste and fashion. On a Sunday I observed the philibeg worn, but not generally. The whole of this delightful place and its environs strongly reminded me of the city of Bonn, on the left bank of the Rhine, known in that romantic region by the name of 'the Little Pearl'.

1815   **Elizabeth Grant of Rothiemurchus**

Memoirs of a Highland Lady

IN JOURNEYING to the highlands we were to sleep at Perth. We reached this pretty town early, and were surprised by a visit from Mr Anderson Blair, a young gentleman possessing property in the Carse of Gowrie, with whom our family had got very intimate during the winter. William was not with us, he had gone on a tour through the west highlands with a very nice person, a College friend, an Englishman. He came to Edinburgh as Mr Shore, rather later than was customary, for he was by no means so young as William and others attending the Classes, but being rich, having no profession, and not College bred, he thought a term or two under our Professors, our University was then deservedly celebrated, would be a very profitable way of passing idle time. Just before he and my brother set out in their tandem with their servants, a second large fortune was left to this favoured son of a mercantile race, for which, however, he had to take the ridiculous name of Nightingale. Mr Blair owed this well sounding addition to the more humble Anderson, born by all the other branches of his large and prosperous family, to the bequest of an old relation. Her legacy was very inferior in amount to the one left to Mr Nightingale, but the pretty estate of Inchyra with a good modern house overlooking the Tay, was part of it, and old John Anderson, the father, was supposed to have died rich. He was therefore a charming escort for my Mother about the town. We had none of us ever seen so much of Perth before. We were taken to sights of all kinds, to shops among the rest, and Perth being famous for whips and gloves, while we admired, Mr Blair bought, and Jane and I were desired to accept a very pretty riding whip each, and a packet of gloves was divided between us. Of course our gallant acquaintance was invited to dinner.

1826-8 **John Ruskin**

Praeterita – Outlines of Scenes and Thoughts Perhaps Worthy of Memory in my Past Life

LAWN AND LAKE ENOUGH indeed I had, in the North Inch of Perth, and pools of pausing Tay, before Rose Terrace, (where I used to live after my uncle died, briefly apoplectic, at Bridge-End), in the peace of the fair Scotch summer days, with my widowed aunt, and my little cousin Jessie, then traversing a bright space between her sixth and ninth year.

But the boys were then all at school or college, – the scholars, William and Andrew, only came home to tease Jessie and me, and eat the biggest jargonel pears; the collegians were wholly abstract; and the two girls and I played in our quiet ways on the North Inch, and by the 'Lead', a stream 'led' from the Tay past Rose Terrace into the town for molinary purposes; and long ago, I suppose, bricked over or choked with rubbish; but then lovely, and a perpetual treasure of flowing diamond to us children. Mary, by the way, was ascending twelve – fair, blue-eyed, and moderately pretty; and as pious as Jessie, without being quite so zealous.

My father rarely stayed with us in Perth, but went on business travels through Scotland, and even my mother became a curiously unimportant figure at Rose Terrace. Mary, Jessie and I were allowed to do what we liked on the Inch: and I don't remember doing any lessons in these Perth times, except the competitive divinity on Sunday.

Had there been anybody then to teach me anything about plants or pebbles, it had been good for me: as it was, I passed my days much as the thistles and tansy did, only with perpetual watching of all the ways of running water, – a singular awe developing itself in me, both of the pools of Tay, where the water changed from brown to blue-black, and of the precipices of Kinnoull; partly out of my own mind, and partly because the servants always became serious when we went up Kinnoull way, especially if I wanted to stay and look at the little crystal spring of Bower's Well.

The dark pools of the Tay were under the high bank at the head of the North Inch, – the path above them being seldom traversed by us children unless at harvest time, when we used to go gleaning in the fields beyond; Jessie and I afterwards grinding our corn in the kitchen pepper-mill, and kneading and toasting for ourselves cakes of pepper bread, of quite unpurchaseable quality. I hesitate, however, in recording as a constant truth for the world, the impression left on me when I went gleaning with Jessie, that Scottish sheaves are more golden than are bound in other lands, and that no harvests elsewhere visible to human eyes are so like the 'corn of heaven' as those of Strath–Tay and Strath–Earn.

1828   **Robert Chambers**

The Picture of Scotland

PERTH, AN ANCIENT royal burgh, a thriving manufacturing town, the metropolis of a large portion of the kingdom, as it once was of the whole, the most beautiful city in Scotland *quoad* situation, and the fourth in point of real elegance, is situated on the left bank of the Tay, about eight-and-twenty miles above its confluence with the sea, and at the distance of forty-four miles from Edinburgh. Occupying the centre of a spacious plain, it is surrounded in every direction by soft and far-stretching declivities, whose sides, thickly ornamented by bower-like villas, hedge it in with a splendid cincture of picturesque and beautiful scenery. Boasting of the most remote antiquity, Perth is hallowed by many delightful old recollections; and it is almost impossible to say whether, by a visit to it, sight or sentiment is most to be gratified.

    Perth consists in two longitudinal old streets, perpendicular to the line of the river, with their adjuncta of *closes* and *gates*, and a number of newer, but scarcely more elegant streets, on both sides. At both sides of the town there are beautiful pieces of public ground for the recreation of the inhabitants, which, having been formerly isolated by the waters of the river, on which they now only border, are respectively called the North and South Inch. A bridge of ten arches, extending over a clear water-way of 590 feet, built in 1772 at an expense of £26,477, connects the city with a suburb called Brigtown, but which is a separate burgh of barony, under the name of Kinnoul.

    The distinguished loveliness of this city, its situation, and the excellence of its schools, have conspired to render it the residence of a great number of affluent idle people, whose influence upon the general population, both as regards their minds and purses, is of course a beneficial one. It is visited, in the summer season, by whole herds of tourists, who never fail to be delighted, as the Romans are said to have been, by the perfect beauty of the scenery around. Pennant called the view from the hill of Moncrieff, where you first come in sight of Perth, in journeying from Edinburgh, 'the Glory of Scotland.' But the conquerers of the world paid it a higher compliment, if all tales be true, by exclaiming, on coming to this point, 'Ecce Tiber! Ecce Campus Martius!'

1828 **Sir Walter Scott**

The Fair Maid of Perth

PERTH, SO EMINENT for the beauty of its situation, is a place of great antiquity, and old tradition assigns to the town the importance of a Roman foundation. That victorious nation, it is said, pretended to recognise the Tiber in the much more magnificent and navigable Tay, and to acknowledge the large level space, well known by the name of the North Inch, as having a near resemblance to their Campus Martius.

> 'Behold the Tiber' the vain Roman cried
> Viewing the ample Tay from Baiglie's side.
> But where's the Scot that would the vaunt repay
> And hail the puny Tiber for the Tay?

...Among all the provinces in Scotland, if an intelligent stranger were asked to describe the most varied and the most beautiful, it is probable he would name the county of Perth. A native also of any other district of Caledonia, though his partialities might lead him to prefer his native county in the first instance, would certainly class that of Perth in the second, and thus give its inhabitants a fair right to plead that, prejudice apart, Perthshire forms the fairest portion of the Northern Kingdom.

...One of the most beautiful points of view which Britain, or perhaps the world, can afford is, or rather we may say was, the prospect from a spot called the Wicks of Baiglie, being a species of niche at which the traveller arrived, after a long stage from Kinross, through a waste and uninteresting country, and from which, as forming a pass over the summit of a ridgy eminence which he had gradually surmounted, he beheld, stretching beneath him, the valley of the Tay, traversed by its ample and lordly stream; the town of Perth, with its two large meadows, or inches, its steeples, and its towers; the hills of Moncrieff and Kinnoul faintly rising into picturesque rocks, partly clothed with woods; the rich margin of the river, studded with elegant mansions; and the distant view of the huge Grampian mountains, the northern screen of this exquisite landscape. The alteration of the road, greatly, it must be owned, to the improvement of general intercourse, avoids this magnificent point of view, and the landscape is introduced more gradually and partially to the eye, though the approach must still be considered as extremely beautiful. There is still, we believe, a footpath left open, by which the station at the Wicks of Baiglie may be approached; and the traveller, by quitting his horse or equipage, and walking a few hundred yards, may still compare the landscape with the sketch we have attempted to give. But it is not in our power to communicate, or in his to receive, the exquisite charm which surprise gives to pleasure, when so splendid a view arises when least expected or hoped for, and which Chrystal Croftangry experienced when he beheld, for the first time, the matchless scene.

Childish wonder, indeed, was an ingredient in my delight, for I was not above fifteen years old; and as this had been my first excursion which I was permitted to make on a pony of my own, I also experienced the glow of independence, mingled with that degree of anxiety which the most conceited boy feels when he is first abandoned to his own undirected counsels. I recollect pulling up the reins without meaning to do so, and gazing on the scene before me as if I had been afraid it would shift like those in a theatre before I could distinctly observe its different parts, or convince myself that what I saw was real. Since that hour, and the period is now more than fifty years past, the recollection of that inimitable landscape has possessed the strongest influence over my mind, and retained its place as a memorable thing, when much that was influential on my own fortunes has fled from my recollection. It is therefore unnatural that, whilst deliberating on what might be brought forward for the amusement of the public, I should pitch upon some narrative connected with the splendid scenery which made so much impression on my youthful imagination, and which may perhaps have that effect in setting off the imperfections of the composition which ladies suppose a fine set of china to possess in heightening the flavour of indifferent tea.

1832–48 **John Dickson**

Reminiscences of Perth Society

MY FIRST EXPERIENCE OF PERTH was in 1832, when I passed through it on my way home to Edinburgh after a tour, along with a cousin, in Argyllshire and Islay, and by Glencoe down the Dochart and Tay to Perth.

My next was in 1836, when I spent a day on my return with my brother from an expedition through Skye, across Ross-shire to Inverness, thence by the side of the Caledonian Canal to the Spean, and by Glenroy, Loch Laggan, and Dalwhinnie to Blair Atholl, where we got the mail. There were neither railways, bicycles, nor motor cars in those days, and young fellows not overburdened with wealth, but endowed with good health and willing to endure fatigue in the pursuit of seeing fine mountain scenery, joyfully attained it on what is popularly known as 'shank's naigie'. We met good friends in Perth by whom we were taken to Craigie Hill and Callerfountain, from which we had a good view of Kilgraston and the lower part of Strathearn. We then took steamer to Dundee, and by another voyaged round the coast of Fife to Leith or Trinity, for Granton was not in existence at that time.

My third visit to Perth was in 1846, with Canadian cousins and two young ladies, on our return from a tour conducted on more luxurious principles. I was the guest of the party, and in the morning I took one of the girls, a pretty Canadian, to show her the Tay in all its grandeur; but she looked over the parapet of the bridge through her gold eyeglass and disposed of the Tay with the remark, 'Ah! A pretty little creek', to which I found it difficult or impossible to make any response in defence.

My next and fourth visit to Perth, in January, 1848, was to be of longer duration, as it has extended to the present time; so that I may be able to say something about it and its inhabitants then and since.

It struck me then, and it does so still, that Perth as a town has little in itself to excite admiration. Though at once regarded as the Capital of Scotland and the residence of its Kings, it is sorely deficient in buildings of any antiquity. The Church of St. John, now divided for three congregations, in the centre of the town, is the only example since the demolition of the Gowrie House, at a period when respect for venerable buildings was at a sad discount. Besides the area of the town is on a very flat level, and not even such spires as then existed had a chance to attract notice. Still less now when so many stalks have risen in the various works and, by their height and smoke have become formidable competitors. The attractions of Perth are in her surroundings – the fine river and its handsome bridge, the two beautiful Inches, and the Hill of Kinnoull looking down on them all, backed by the Grampians, from Ben Voirlich to the Spittal of Glenshee.

I don't think that there was much change on the town itself between my first visit in 1832 and my fourth in 1848. In the early part of the nineteenth century a good deal had been done, and the old Royalty, a little scrap of a place, had been put into a new casing, especially on its north and south sides facing the two Inches – Rose Terrace and Atholl Crescent and Place on the north, and Marshall Place on the south; but after that effort there had been an entire cessation from further exertion, and the community seemed content to rest upon their laurels in the way of building. The municipal body, under an Act of Parliament, directed their attention to the improvement of the navigation of the Tay, with the hope of making Perth a great commercial centre. In this they were unfortunate, for at the same time the railway system had begun, and in ten years, after their operations were completed, they had to face the competition and rivalry of the Perth and Dundee line, and, like all canals and communications by inland water, they had no chance of success.

It was in the spring of 1848 that the line to Dundee from Barnhill was completed and opened, and the general talk of everybody was about railways and the wonderful results to follow from them.

1836   George Penny

Names from the First Perth Directory

THE ARISTOCRACY
Two Kings and one Queen,
Two Dukes and one Marquis,
One Earl and two Barons,
Two Nobles and two Knights,
Two Bishops and three Deans,

Three Chapels and six Chaplains,
Two Gentry and three Squires,
Three Bailies and four Justices,
Three Lairds and one Tennant,
Four Farmers and one Cottar,
Three Merchants and one Couper.

THE MOBOCRACY

Two Banks and three Braes, Three Crows and five Keays,
Three Hills and one Glen, Four Mounts and one Plane,
Four Hoggs and three Herds, Two Lambs and three Kidds,
One Cross and three Dodds, Two Hares and five Todds,
Two Dowies and one Wann, Two Herons and one Swan,
Seven Youngs and three Aulds, Four Grays and two Balds,
Two Waters and three Fords, One Gunn and four Swords,
One Cant and one Will, One Drinkwater and one Gill,
One Maltman and four Brewsters, Thirty Taylors
        and three Shewsters,
Two Bowes and one Bandy, Three Dons and one Dandie,
Two Macleans and two Macfeats, One Cole and two Peats,
One Law and two Lynches, Four Myles and two Inches,
Two Condies and one Shore, A hundred Stewarts
        and one More,
One Bone and one Stone, one Adam quite alone.

Traditions of Perth

NEW YEAR'S DAY has always been held in Perth as a day of special hilarity. The festivities commenced on the evening of the last night of the old year. In addition to a sufficient supply of stimulants, each family provided a quantity of carls. These were oatmeal cakes of a triangular shape, prepared with treacle or other condiments. The whole circle of acquaintance visited for carls: and each individual had to sing for his supper, or at least for his cake. This practice has greatly fallen off: none but a rabble of children, called "Guisards", now maintain the custom. New Year's morning was ushered in by a dram from the gudewife's bottle. It was then the practice to wait up for what was called the cream of the well – the fortunate damsel who succeeded in getting the first water of the year, being assured of a good husband before the end of it. The streets were crowded all night, by parties wishing to see what was going on, and by others on their way to call upon acquaintances. The ordinary restraints of society were thrown aside; and every man claimed the privilege of kissing any woman he chanced to meet. To this ancient and edifying practice, the whisky bottle came to be added, and the oblations of Bacchus were offered at the shrine of Venus.

The changes which took place in trade about 1780, brought a great number of spinners and cloth printers to this neighbourhood, who introduced the custom of hot pints. On going to the houses of their friends, as first foot, they took with them a tea kettle full of a warm mixture of ale, whisky and sugar; and as the visitor had also to do honour to the host's bottle, the paties, long before daylight, found they had taken more than enough.

Handsel Monday was the principal day with the working classes. By one in the morning the streets were in an uproar with young people, who appeared to consider themselves privileged to do whatever mischief they pleased.

It was a constant practice to pull down sign boards, or any thing that came in the way, and make a large bonfire with them at the cross, – all being for the benefit of trade, and the support of the good old customs. Numbers of boys, belonging to the Glover Incorporation, were to be heard in every quarter selling small purses at a half-penny each; they were made of the pairings of leather, and enabled the lads to gather something to hold Handsel Monday with. They were generally all sold off early in the morning. The tradesmen were all idle this day, and considered themselves entitled to handsel from their employers; and even from individuals in any way connected with the business. Thus the weavers, having received their handsel from the manufacturer, a deputation was sent to the wright who made their utensils; another to the reed-maker, and to the chandler who supplied them with candles; and a third to the company who boiled the yarn. The whole proceeds of these begging commissions were put together and spent in the evening in a tavern.

Formerly, Christmas, as a period of festivity, was but little attended to, excepting among the Episcopalians. Latterly, as the above customs declined among the operatives, parties among the higher and middling classes, during the Christmas holidays, have rapidly increased.

1837 Dr Thomas Frognall Dibdin

Bibliographical, Antiquarian and Picturesque Tour in the Northern Counties of England and Scotland

ON DESCENDING FROM THE HEIGHTS, the whole town has a fine aspect, reminding me, I know not why, of the smart, cheerful air of a provincial town in England. A broad and noble bridge of stone bestrides the River Tay. To the right is a beautiful racecourse of rich turf, enfiladed by the river, and having to the left some fine street scenery. But what most struck me, on my first approach to Perth – descending from the upper road to Kinfauns Castle – was the Water Works, of which Professor Anderson had both the construction and direction. Here was a lesson to learn – or a model to copy – for all England. Here was deformity converted into beauty, and a nuisance rendered a picturesque accessory.

1840 **Lord Henry Thomas Cockburn**

From his Journals

WE WERE IN COURT all Friday and yesterday; and this has been a well spent day. For I have been round the North Inch, I cannot tell how often, and at the top of Kinnoull Hill, and had a pleasant, quiet dinner of eight, and have enjoyed this rose of country towns, from morning to night, from the dewy grass of before breakfast to the serene moon at twelve at night.

...There should be Cities of Refuge. Hence the envy which it is said that Perth sometimes has of Dundee, is nearly inconceivable. One would have thought that there was no Perth man (out of the asylum) who would not have rejoiced in his unsustained tranquility, in the delightful heights that enclose him, – in his silvery Tay, – in the quiet beauty of his green and level Inches. Yet it is said that some of them actually long for steam engines on Kinnoull Hill, and docks, and factories, and the sweets of the Scouring burn. But I do not believe this. It is incredible. Long may both they and we be spared.

1842 **Queen Victoria**

From her Highland Journals

TUESDAY, SEPTEMBER 6

We changed horses next at the Bridge of Earn (twelve miles). At half-past three we reached Dupplin, Lord Kinnoull's. All the time the views of the hills, and dales, and streams were lovely. The last part of the road very bad travelling, up and down hill. Dupplin is a very fine modern house with a very pretty view of the hills on one side, and a small waterfall close to the front of the house. A battalion of the 42nd Highlanders was drawn up before the house, and the men looked very handsome in their kilts. We each received an address from the nobility and gentry of the country, read by Lord Kinnoull; and from the Provost and Magistrates of Perth. We then lunched. The Willoughbys, Kinnairds, Ruthvens, and Lord Mansfield, and one of his sisters, with others, were there. After luncheon, we walked a little way in the grounds, and then at five o'clock we set off again. We very soon came upon Perth, the situation of which is quite lovely; it is on the Tay, with wooded hills skirting it entirely on one side, and hills are seen again in the distance, the river winding beautifully.

Albert was charmed, and said it put him in mind of the situation of Basle. The town itself (which is very pretty) was immensely crowded, and the people very enthusiastic; triumphal arches had been erected in various places. The Provost presented me with the keys, and Albert with the freedom of the city. Two miles beyond is Scone (Lord Mansfield's), a fine-looking house of reddish stone.

Lord Mansfield and the dowager Lady Mansfield received us at the door, and took us to our rooms, which were very nice.

Wednesday, September 7

We walked out, and saw the mound on which the ancient Scotch kings were always crowned; also the old arch with James VI's arms, and the old cross, which is very interesting.

Before our windows stands a sycamore-tree planted by James VI. A curious old book was brought to us from Perth, in which the last signatures are those of James I (of England) and of Charles I, and we were asked to write our names in it, and we did so. Lord Mansfield told me yesterday that there were some people in the town who wore the identical dresses that had been worn in Charles I's time. At eleven o'clock we set off as before. We drove through part of Perth and had a very fine view of Scone. A few miles on, we passed the field of the battle of Luncarty, where tradition says the Danes were beaten by Lord Erroll's ancestor.

1847   **John Ruskin**

From his Diaries

AUGUST 25TH. WEDNESDAY. DUNKELD. I passed through Perth to-day; nineteen years since I was there, and I am very sad tonight. It came on dark at 10 and remained grey all day, a shower coming on just as we entered by the South Inch. All looked hopeless and cheerless; the town smoky and ugly in outer suburbs; the Bowerswell houses crowded and the ground behind ragged. And yet I thought Glen Farg and the hill of Moncreiff as lovely as ever, allowing for the desperate change in *me* – but Perth not. And I have had the saddest walk this afternoon I ever had in my life. Partly from my own pain in not seeing E(uphemia) G(ray) and in far greater degree, as I found by examining it thoroughly, from thinking that my own pain was perhaps much less than hers, not knowing what I know. And all this with a strange deadly shadow over everything, such as I hardly would comprehend; I expected to be touched by it, which I was not, but then came a horror of great darkness – not distress, but cold, fear and gloom. I am a little better now. After all, when the feelings have been so deadened by long time, I do not see how the effect on them can be anything else than this.

1849   **Queen Victoria**

From her Highland Journals

TUESDAY, AUGUST 14

We passed Stirling in the distance, and a little before four we reached Perth, where the people were very friendly. We took the children in our carriage and drove straight to the 'George Inn', where we had the same rooms that we had last time.

Albert went out immediately to see the prison, and at six we drove together along the London Road (as they rather strangely call it), towards Moncrieffe. The view was perfectly beautiful, and is the finest of Perth and the grand bridge over the Tay.

1863 **Lucy Parker**

From her Diary Describing her Family's Holiday in Scotland

ONE FINE VIEW from the bridge and heaps and heaps of dirty tattered children, with white hair and bare legs, rolling, sprawling or squalling in the mud and washing in the gutter. We had had quite enough of Perth in twenty minutes and returned by the next train.

1869 **The Reverend Samuel Ferguson**

The Queen's Visit and Other Poems

THE QUEEN'S VISIT (*An extract*)
Still on the Royal progress speeds,
By hill and dale they wind,
Till needed rest and welcome cheer,
'Neath Dupplin's tow'rs they find.

Still on they press till Perth is reached,
That ancient city fair,
Where royal lips in thousands join
To cheer the Royal pair.

The good old town revives again
Beneath the royal tread;
Its ancient glories start to view,

And courtly life long dead.

To Scone proud Scotland's honour'd Queen
With joyous heart proceeds;
To Scone – historic Scone – grown old
In brave and kingly deeds.

Its palace boasts historic fame;
Its site is sacred ground;
For there for ages all our kings
In solemn state were crowned.

The Royal chair, as aged bards
Have dared to dream and sing
Is sacred still to Kenneth's line -
That ancient Scottish King.

Though now its marble seat adorns
Westminster's holy fane,
'Tis still the coronation chair
For Britain's wide domain.

At ancient Scone the Royal guests
With Mansfield's lord abode
One passing eve – then has'ning on,
They took the Highland road.

Lord Mansfield rode, the Queen beside,
Imparting ancient lore,
And pointing out with patriot pride
Those spots renown'd of yore.

The grand North Inch is pass'd, where knights
In tourney oft have played –
There stood the lists – and here apart,
The King the scene survey'd.

There too, at times, the battle notes
Rang out with clarion tone,
And stalwart men rush'd down on death,
In those dark ages gone.

The Royal progress, speeding on,
Is viewed by joyous eyes;
At every turn, on every side,
The shouts of welcome rise.

With loyal shouts they voice their love,
And cheer her on her way;
The Grampian hills, now quite at hand,
How proud they look to-day!

c.1870 **William Clyde**

Craigie Hill

The praise of Yarrow, Teviot, Tweed,
Ben Lomond's height, Gleniffer's dell;
Of Lugar, Irvine, Ayr and Doon,
Our woodland echoes often tell.
'Mid matchless grandeur, rich and gay,
Muse of the North! Then say, why still
Unsung the glorious banks of Tay,
And sunny slopes of Craigie Hill?

Tay's 'combinations of bright scenes
Breathe music' – then no more be mute.
Whilst thousand rhymes on meaner floods
Aid shepherd's pipe or lover's lute.
Sons of our mountains, ever brave –
Maids of our glens – though chaste not chill –
These be thy theme, with banks of Tay,
And sunny slopes of Craigie Hill.

The Romans, following from afar
Agricola to northern wars,
In Tay and its fair banks beheld
Their Tiber and their Field of Mars.
That landscape stopped the veterans' march
Till admiration gazed its fill;
Their shouts resound along the Tay,
And up the slopes of Craigie Hill.

Those shouts soon roused, o'er many a glen,
The Caledonians in their pride –
'If worthy conquest, then our land
Is worth defence!' they fiercely cried.
Italia's soldiers bit the dust,
Their red blood died the mountain rill;
A thinn'd, desponding band recross'd
The sunny slopes of Craigie Hill.

Are not yon fair fields Luncarty?
Is not St Johnstoun at our feet?
Where Dane and Southron our bold sires
In the death struggle dared to meet:
Whence Charlie march'd his scanty band –

For kingdoms three struck with a will;
They failed, although with gallant hearts
They left the slopes of Craigie Hill.

And in our time, when Britain stood
Against a banded world alone,
From the Unconquerable Isle
The noblest of her youth were gone;
Lads of crisp locks and bearing free
Tay sent, resolved their blood to spill,
Ere alien flag should float above
The sunny slopes of Craigie Hill.

Roll on, proud Tay, by tower and town,
Amid thy gorgeous scenery;
Aye be thy Strath unequalled for
Luxuriant fertility.
The dwellers on thy banks the Muse
Has sung. One part awaits her skill –
To chant thy beauties as they lie
View'd from the slopes of Craigie Hill.

1870   **Malcolm Ferguson**

A Tour Through The Highlands of Perthshire

ABOUT NINE O'CLOCK we arrived at the ancient city of Perth, long the capital of Scotland, and the scene of many tragic and important historical events.

The spacious railway station was crowded to excess. It happened to be the Prince Albert Annual Holiday, duly kept by the Perth folks, in commemoration of the uncovering of the Prince Albert

Statue, erected in 1864, and situated at the lower end of the North Inch, facing Charlotte Street. The only inscription on it is simply 'Albert, 1864.'

A large number of people were leaving the Fair City per special trains for the Birnam Games.

Having left our traps at the left luggage office in the station, and being in rare trim for a gude substantial breakfast, we at once steered for the British Hotel (Pople's), a large house close to the station; and while discussing breakfast, I ordered 'white-choker' to bespeak a drosky for us, which, on coming out after breakfast, we found waiting for us. It was an open, one-horse, and by far the best turn-out, including both Jehu and horse, baith being real weel faured, and like their meat and meal, that we got during our trip. Driving through the principal streets of the city, we crossed the Tay, which is here spanned by a rather narrow but splendid bridge of ten arches, and extends over a clear waterway of about 600 feet. The entire length of the bridge is about 890 feet. It was opened in 1772. I was glad to find that there was nae toll to pay. The former bridges were at four successive periods carried away by heavy floods, and, from 1621 until the completion of the present bridge, communication across the river was maintained solely by a ferry. After crossing the bridge, we thence steered in the direction of Kinnoull Hill, probably about two miles or thereabouts from our starting point. The road ascends a very steep brae, and on arriving at the verge of the woods which crown the higher parts of the hill, we discharged our respectable-looking Coachee and his braw mare Jess, and found ourselves in front of a neat cottage, occupied by the guide who accompanies strangers to the top of the hill, about half-a-mile or so distant from the cottage, up a zig-zag road through the thick woods.

The guide – I omitted to 'speer' his name – was sittin' afore his cottage door, and on our approach he at once prepared to accompany us. I was rather struck at first sight with his appearance, pretty well up in years, probably about half way between fifty and sixty, very tall and muscular-looking, but not overly burdened with either flesh or fat. He had a strong bristling beard, and, from the way it had been clippit, it was quite evident its owner wasna at all particular as to its shape or style. He had a peculiar stammer or impediment in his speech; and, whether caused by rheumatism, or some other of the many ills frail mortal man is heir to, I couldna say, but his right knee-joint was very stiff, and I am not quite sure but the right leg might be a wee bit shorter than the other. He made use of a stout rung o' a staff. I soon discovered that our wisest policy, while in his company, was just to let him have his own way, and no thwart him, as it appeared to me very evident that our new-found freen was rather a cross-grained auld carle, and had been accustomed to tell his stories in his ain way, without being called too much in question. On gaining a bare spot on the very summit of the hill, we were amply repaid for our toil by the magnificent panoramic prospect that burst on our admiring gaze.

I have stood on the highest pinnacle of some of our loftiest Bens, from which no doubt the view is very grand, but consists not unfrequently chiefly of a hazy sea of surrounding mountains, and perhaps a few lakes appearing like silver specks amidst the far-stretching dreary waste of corries, glens, and scarred and rugged mountains.

The view from Kinnoull Hill – generally reckoned the finest in Scotland – is more varied and pleasing to the eye. To the north or north-west Kinnoull descends in a steep acclivity to the river, and on the south by a range of rocky precipices of considerable height. Nestled at the base of these precipices, almost immediately below where we stand, are seen Kinfauns Castle, and some other country seats, and beautifully wooded slopes, falling gradually into the famous Carse of Gowrie, stretching away eastwards towards Dundee.

The Fair City itself lies on a level plain on the west bank of the Tay, and in a rather compact mass at our feet – the North and South

Inches occupying either side of the city, along the bank of the Tay. The Perth Penitentiary, an extensive building, is seen on the south side of the South Inch, erected in 1812, and then used as a depot for French prisoners, of whom it could accommodate from 7000 to 8000.

A great number of railway lines are seen from this point. The screams of the steam-whistles are constantly heard, and curling wreaths of white vapour are seen approaching at a dashing pace from almost every point of the compass – all converging to the Perth Joint Station, and forming a peculiar feature in the surrounding landscape – the Perth and Dundee line from the east; the Kinross line from the south; the Stirling and Glasgow line from the south-west; the Crieff and Methven line from the west; the Highland line from the north; the Aberdeen line from the north-east.

On returning to the guide's cottage we rested for some time, and one of our party got a small refreshment. The day was very hot, but bright and clear; and, after 'a gude lang crack,' we parted with our guide on the best o' terms; and I have no doubt his bark is waur than his bite, and that he is true at the core.

On our way down the hill we stepped off the road for a hundred yards or so to inspect an elegant Roman Catholic church which was in course of being finished. Adjoining the church is a handsome building – a home for aged priests – at least I was so informed. This really fine church and building, situated high up the hill side, are very prominent objects from the Fair City, which it overlooks. Re-crossing the bridge, we strolled through the town; but the shops, &c., being all closed, it had a somewhat dull appearance.

The principal edifices are the County Buildings, a very elegant porticoed structure, fronting the Tay, between the bridge and South Inch, on the site of the Gowrie House, handed down to fame by the Gowrie Conspiracy. The most ancient, the most largely connected with historical associations, is the Church of St John's, originally called the 'Kirk of the Holy Cross of St John the Baptist.' It stands in an open space on the west side of St John Street. It was in this church where John Knox preached his celebrated sermon against popery and monasteries.

We gazed with much interest on three statues, situated in different parts of the town, viz, Prince Albert, Sir Walter Scott and his favourite greyhound, and Robert Burns.

After paying a brief visit to the British Hotel, we proceeded to the railway station, where we spent some time admiring its admirable arrangements for the convenience and comfort of passengers. It is the most elegant, spacious, and commodious station in Scotland, if not in Britain. The passenger shed alone covers an area of 88,110 square feet, besides a large covered space for engines &c., and everything is kept in first-rate order. The ticket offices in connection with the respective lines starting from this station appear remarkably well arranged and complete.

1883   **Paxton Hood**

Scottish Characteristics

AND WE REMEMBER to have met with an anecdote of a Scotchman from Perth, who had penetrated into some far interior of Asia – we forget where; he had to see the Pasha, or Bashaw. He was introduced to the comely man in his tent. They gathered up their knees, and sat down upon their carpets. They drank their strong coffee, and smoked their hookahs together in common silence; few words, at any rate passed between them, but, we may trust, sufficient for the occasion; but when the man of Perth was about to leave, the Pasha also arose, and, following him outside the tent, said, in good strong Doric Scotch, 'I kenned ye verra weel in Perth; ye are just sae and sae.' The Perth man was astonished, as well he might be, until the Pasha explained, as he said, 'I'm just a Perth man mysel'!' He had travelled, and he had become of importance to the Government there. His story was not very creditable. In the expectation of the post he filled, he had become a Mohammedan. But he was an illustration of the ubiquity of his race.

1886 The Reverend Samuel Gosnell Green

Scotland 100 Years Ago

AUCHTERARDER is next passed, a name once famous in ecclesiastical controversy; and the train traverses a broad valley until it rolls into the wide echoing station of PERTH. The 'fair city,' however, need not detain us. Its far-famed Inches are broad level meadows. Kinnoul Hill is beautiful for its wooded walks and for its fine views towards the Grampian Mountains, while the Carse of Gowrie, an expanse of rich meadow-land bordering the Tay, stretches eastward, and the blue waters of the estuary gleam beyond. It is said that Moncrieff Hill, on the other side of the river, is equally fine; but I had no time to ascend both, or rather, as the time of visit happened to be the Sabbath evening after the services of the day, it was more congenial to rest, in quiet talk with a friend, as together we watched the sunset over the distant hills.

Returning to the railway station in the morning, we find two sets of trains bound for the Highlands. One is by Forfar to Aberdeen and the east; the other by Blair Athole more directly northward.

*　*　*

c.1890 **Francis Buchanan**

Kinnoull Cliff

Romantic scene! once more from thy proud steep,
Kinnoull, I view the prospect far below;
Stirr'd with the memories of the past I weep,
As in my fancy boyhood's pleasures grow;
Even now I feel as I felt long ago.

Far down beneath me, in the vernal sun,
Majestic Tay, impatient to be free,
Rolls his broad waters, sparkling as they run
Thro' many a lovely spot, towards the sea;
And at this height methinks I hear their minstrelsy.

Full many a happy hour I've roamed, I ween,
On yonder dappled banks in days of yore,
Watching at even the silvery Lunar beam,
And the crimp'd ripple plashing on the shore;
But those gay hours are dead – the past returns no more.

Kinfauns, thy castle peers amid the trees,
The turrets gilded as with burnished gold;
The crimson standard waving in the breeze
As it was wont when Longueville the bold
With his retainers fought the Southron 'neath its fold.

And thou, forlorn Elcho, famed in lore
For gallant deeds of noble Wallace wight,
Whose patriot fame is known on every shore;
His mighty arm asserted Scotia's right,
And led her hardy sons triumphant thro' the fight.

Now thy grey walls are crumbling fast away,
And mould'ring ruin seizes thee amain.
These moss-grown gaps tell of Time's potent sway,
And the green woodbine, with its creeping train,
Seems to protect from waste thy tott'ring form in vain.

Dark Moredun, too, rears up his furrow'd head,
Where, long ago, Rome's legions from afar
Swept o'er his craggy heights with thund'rous tread,
Equipp'd in all the barbarous pomp of war –
The spear, the sword and buckler, horse and rattling car.

Far as mine eye can reach the verdant plain
Displays its gorgeous beauty, rich, serene.
There rears a noble mansion, here again
A clump of lowly cottages is seen,
With woods, green fields, and rivers interspersed between.

Oh, Scotland! land of peace and happiness,
Of all the climes of this old earth the best:
Beneath thy soil, scenes of my early bliss,
I pray to Heaven my weary bones may rest,
Where oft in boyhood's day my foot the heath hath prest.

Farewell, ye rocky steeps! Sweet Tay, farewell!
Ye woods, ye wilds, and solitudes, adieu!
I may not e'er again (ah, who can tell?)
Thus feast mine eyes upon this matchless view,
Life's but a flickering light – our days are number'd few.

* * *

1891 **John Geddie**

Illustrations of the Scenery of the River Tay

THE BRIMMING, DIMPLING volume of water that rolls along so evenly under the many arches of the Bridge of Perth, and fills the whole space of two or three hundred yards interposing between the North Inch and the steep bank covered by the villas of Bridgend, seems incapable of being roused into wrath or haste. The scene around it – as wide and rich and fair a landscape as the heart of man could desire – framed in by the encircling hills, and embracing the charms of country and of town subdued into marvellous harmony, appears, when seen in the quiet summer evening, to be touched by a peace which has not been disturbed for ages. Yet the North Inch, and the approaches to the Bridge, have often heard the clash of angry steel; Tay itself has rushed past red and furious as if all the turbulent passions of the hillmen, and not the serene peace of the hills, were gathered in its breast.

The shadow of the olden time seems to brood over the woods of Scone, and to soften and darken the background of the scene, as viewed from the Bridge of Perth. Near at hand the picture is both fair and bright. The wide rippled mirror of the Tay separates the group of houses gathered about Bridgend – the tall poplars and umbrageous limes and planes by the water-side, succeeded by fields and by pine and beech woods that climb to the summit of Kinnoull Hill – from the green Inches and the noble line of buildings with which the Fair City fronts the river. Whatever judgment may be formed of its interior – which, it must be confessed, is not devoid of squalor – Perth, viewed from without, is still one of the most beautiful of towns. Few cities, pitched as this is in a valley bottom, have such advantages of seeing and of being seen. On one side the placid and ample Tay; on other two sides the open and breezy North Inch, and the shady walks and glades of the South Inch; towards the west gently rising uplands, diversified by fields and woods, behind which are drawn the softly pencilled outlines of the distant hills, it cannot be said that Perth is hampered or obstructed in its outlook. Gazing round on it from the Bridge, or better still, looking down on it from its neighbouring heights, one can easily understand how the place came to be chosen for a time as the centre of the national and ecclesiastical life of Scotland, and how in more troublous days Court and Council had to desert it for a safer nest. Now that peace and wealth, 'gamyn and glee', have settled down on Scotland, Perth draws more powerfully than ever by the force of its beauty. The streams of Highland tourist traffic meet and eddy round the 'cross of St. Johnstoun': and in the early weeks of August they rise in spate.

Doubtless the citizens of Perth now regret their unthrift haste in using the besom of improvement to sweep away the memorials of its past. It was famous among Scottish cities for the number and wealth of its monastic houses. Not a trace of them is to be found, unless it be a dubious fragment of convent wall or a name on a street corner. The Reformation began the work of destruction, and no later revulsion of public taste or feeling in favour of the old occurred to arrest it.

1892   **Beatrix Potter**

From her Journal

WEDNESDAY, JULY 27TH – Reached Perth about seven o'clock in the morning, and washed in uncommonly cold water. Got the *Scotsman* and also copy of preceding day's issue with caustic comments on Carnegie's strike.

There was an extraordinary miscellaneous scramble in the first-class restaurant-room at Perth. A hard, hairy Scotcher opposite doing it thoroughly in five courses, porridge, salmon, cutlets, chops, ham and eggs and marmalade. Under my chair a black retriever and on my left a large man in knickerbockers, facing a particularly repulsive Scotch mother and young baby feeding on sops. All the company extremely dirty and the attendants inattentive.

I don't think the new Station at Perth is an improvement at all, except in handsomeness. I remember the old first-class waiting room with a rather greedy relish as a child. It was one of the rare occasions when one was allowed to eat ham and eggs. From the arrangement of the local trains in those days, we had several hours in Perth, a leisurely interval in the middle of the remove.

There used to be a large dingy-coloured panel of the Royal Arms, in the old refreshment room which I looked upon with awe. The company was quaint and highly flavoured. I remember one objectionable old gentleman with a bald head and greasy wisps of hair, tied on the top thereof in a knot. The only familiar survival in the new Station is little Martin.

Arrived at Birnam station about eight. We took possession of Heath Park, which in spite of its fine name, is a Villa, well-built, but in disrepair, standing in one acre of ground.

TUESDAY, SEPTEMBER 13TH – To Perth with papa, the first time I have been on the railway since we have been here, which I consider shabby. I enjoyed it extremely. It was very showery and the corn all drowned, a sad sight on the fine rolling land about Luncarty and Strathord.

Perth was uncommonly cold and draggled. My new boots which hurt, conveniently got wet through shortly, and papa stood me another pair, two pairs in one year, 'Oh Gemini', but this latest pair are very comfortable.

Had a large lunch for ten-pence. 'Cookies', 'Bridies' and lemonade at Woods, two nice merry lasses who advised us to the shoemakers, whose name by a coincidence was also Wood. I was looking at the younger one's hair, how quickly fashions spread, the loose mane and habit is as curious in contagion as the influenza.

Perth in the new parts is a well-built town, plenty of good reddish stone, and the side streets are very wide and deserted, paved with cobbles, and much grass grown like the streets of Edinburgh.

We went along the North Inch, admiring the little gardens full of flowers. Passed a very large hideous new Free Church, a barbarous mixture of gothic and castellated architecture. We saw a second large Free Church.

The shops are good, especially the drapers. There are a great many cats. The wynds and lower back parts of the city are most noisome, indeed the Scotch are a filthy people, their main idea of the use of a running stream is to carry off what they call *refuse*.

Every burn that passes a farm has its jaw-hole, serving as an ashpit. At Dunkeld the town rubbish is shot below the Bridge, and at Perth we were shocked at the volume of black liquid pouring out of several large sewer arches.

The beautiful white gulls pounce on the garbage and are remarkably tame. An old man was throwing them bits of bread for which they darted, screaming, dropping it and soaring again.

The railings are extremely rickety, people are constantly drowned, but there is a sluttish carelessness of life. Witness the universal habit of walking on the line. There have been two run over between here and Blair this summer, but the Fiscal looks at them and they are put underground without more ado.

From Perth Bridge we looked over at the river coming down in spate, at the corner of the North Inch below us, a knot of men and a brown and white dog pulled out a dead sheep, but, upon consideration, launched it again with a boat-hook.

The Museum was shut. I looked in at the shop windows at the photographs of Perth. Miss Julia Neilson, probably on tour, Mr Balfour, sundry Law Lords, and often the Duke of Clarence with poor Princess May. Poor lady, an attractive face, but I doubt if very correct features, the eyes and nose too sharp, the mouth large, not so pretty as her mother is represented to have been, and with the same tendency to stoutness, but her photographs do not do her appearance justice.

The Scotch are an odd mixture of sentiment and hard sense. They would have more affection for the very worst of Stuart Kings than the very best of Guelphs, but no one could suspect them of the faintest sympathy with a second '45 if a Pretender existed, but they have no affection whatever for the present Royal Family. Sir W. Gordon Cumming is idolised further north.

They are eminently suitable for intellectual Republicans with modern Athens ready to hand, completely competent to manage their own affairs, according to their own lights.

The city is boiling over with indignation because some extraneous Inspector has informed them and the world, that they are poisoning themselves with drinking the water of the Tay.

The main object of our visit to Perth was to see a miscellaneous collection of old furniture, and odds and ends got together at Brady's the Auctioneers. There was less absolute rubbish than usual, though of course a compliment to call it Chippendale. Some stiff, high-backed armchairs, that would be very useful to an artist.

The swords were very good, a real Andrea Ferrara, it sold for £7, a Charles Mortuary sword, some rusty old bucket-hilted broadswords, and an amazing blunderbuss. We fingered the swords consideringly, but they were spikish.

We put in for two Lots of China and got the wrong one, much sneezed at since brought home, but I foresee a certain bowl of little Nankeen will be to me a joy for ever – until it breaks – cheap at a pound. I may even get the money back. I make the most of my few properties.

The 'about 250 ancient copper coins' comprised so many duplicates we made no offer, though, had I been present at the actual sale, I would have bid a shilling or two for the sake of the bad ones!, the counterfeit Hanover sovereign amongst them. Precious little copper.

It is rather curious if you secure a lot by proxy, it is secured at the very exact sum you name. We got hold of a very uninteresting stupid man in an apron, whose mind appeared to be a blank.

We wandered along Tay Street looking over at the gulls, and dived into a deserted looking frame shop, with a paper on the door-pull, requesting customers to go round to High Street if it was fast. There was a very chatty, elderly foreman in the workshop, who cut cardboard mounts to admiration, discussing meanwhile the merits of a little green bull canary, and the misfortunes of German competition, and the eight-hour question.

There was a stack of gilt moulding for frames from Germany as a matter of course. He was so civil as to teach me how to draw a correct oval with two pins and a bit of string, very ingenious and useful.

We had to hurry to catch our train. Met a fine Clydesdale stallion passing along. There is an extraordinary multitude of cows, perhaps a hundred, grazing on the Inch, all sorts and conditions.

The statue of Scott is very bad, but it was a pleasant thought to set it there, and a favourite perching-place for doves. I met *Gow Crom* a few steps farther, leading a cart of coals, and could not help smiling to think how a realistic modern writer would have spoiled a pretty picture, and explained the inexplicable reluctance of '*The Fair Maid of Perth*'.

THURSDAY, SEPTEMBER 15TH – Being too showery to photograph, papa went to Perth again, picked up the China and called on the Millais', encamped with old Mrs Gray. Their house is rebuilt.

* * *

| 1894 | **The Reverend Dr Andrew K. H. Boyd** |

On Returning from Strathpeffer to St Andrews
and Changing Trains at Perth for Dundee

THE MISERABLE DISORGANISATION of Perth Station
must be seen to be understood. The staff of porters was sadly deficient.
Not one could be had, even by liberal bribery. One or two men set in
authority were quite the stupidist human beings I have ever seen. The
train, of course, was much too late. And when my wife had pitifully
struggled over the bridge to the Dundee train, carrying a weight for
which she was quite unequal, my hands were much more than full too,
it was to see the train move off. I trust I may never see that deplorable
station or its bemuddled servants in this world again.

| 1894 | **William McGonagall** |

Extracts from the Autobiography of
William McGonagall

WELL, MY DEAR FRIENDS, the next event in my life
that I am going to relate is regarding me and my Mistress McGonagall
leaving Dundee in the year 1894, resolving to return no more owing
to the harsh treatment I had received in the city as is well known for a
truth without recording it. Well, I went to the Fair City of Perth, one
of the finest upon the earth, intending to remain there altogether. So I
secured a small garret in the South Street, and me and my mistress
lived there for eight months, and the inhabitants were very kind to us
in many respects.

...My dear readers – I must now tell ye my reason for leaving
the Fair City of Perth. It was because I found it too small for me for
making a living in. I must allow, the inhabitants were very kind to me
during my stay amongst them. And while living there I received a letter,

and when I opened it I was struck by amazement when I found a silver elephant enclosed, and I looked at it in amazement, and said - 'I'll now have a look at the big letter enclosed.' I was amazed to see that King Theebaw of Burmah and Andaman Islands, had conferred upon me the honorary title of Sir Wm. Topaz McGonagall, Knight of the White Elephant of Burmah.

The City of Perth

Beautiful ancient City of Perth,
One of the fairest on the earth,
With your stately mansions and scenery most fine,
Which seems very beautiful in the summer time;
And the beautiful silvery Tay,
Rolling smoothly on its way,
And glittering like silver in the sunshine –
And the Railway Bridge across it is really sublime.
The scenery is very beautiful when in full bloom,
It far excels the river Doon –
For the North Inch and South Inch is
    most beautiful to behold,
Where the buttercups do shine in the sunshine like gold.

And there's the Palace of Scone, most beautiful to be seen,
Near by the river Tay and the North Inch so green,
Whereon is erected the statue of Prince Albert,
    late husband to the Queen,
And also the statue of Sir Walter Scott is most
    beautiful to be seen,
Erected on the South Inch, which would please the Queen,
And recall to her memory his novels she has read –

And came her to feel a pang for him that is dead.
Beautiful City of Perth, along the river Tay,
I must conclude my lay,
And to write in praise of thee my heart does not gainsay,
To tell the world fearlessly, without the least dismay –
With your stately mansions and the beautiful river Tay,
You're one of the fairest Cities of the present day.

The Fair Maid of Perth's House

All ye good people, afar and near,
To my request pray lend an ear;
I advise you all without delay to go
And see the Fair Maid's House – it is a rare show.

Some of the chairs there are very grand,
They have been cut and carved by a skilful hand;
An kings, perchance, if the truth be told,
Have sat on them in days of old.

King James the First of Scotland was murdered there*,
And his cries for mercy rent the air.
But the Highland robbers only laughed at him,
And murdered him in the dungeon and thought of no sin.

Then there's an shrine upstairs,
Where the Monks and Saints said their prayers,
To the Holy Virgin, be it told;
And the house, it is said, is six hundred years old.

The old cruisie lamps are there to be seen,

Which let the monks see to write from their sheen,
And if the walls could speak, they would tell a fearful tale,
Which would make the people's cheeks turn pale.

Then there's an old claymore dug up from Culloden Moor,
Which in its time shed innocent blood, I am sure,
If not at Culloden Moor, some other place,
Which no doubt the truth of it history might trace.

The interior of the house is magnificent to be seen,
And the wood panelling, I'm sure, would please the Queen;
And the old fire-place, with its big fire,
Is all that visitors could desire.

Then there's a ring in a big stone near by the door,
Where gentlemen tethered their horses in days of yore;
And on the staircase door there's a firling pin
For making a rattling noise when anyone wanted in.

The mistress of the house is very kind,
A more affable woman would be hard to find;
And to visitors she is very good,
And well versed in history, be it understood.

Although the Fair Maid's House is one of the oldest in Perth, it was not the scene of James I's assassination, or any of the medieval occurrences described by McGonagall. The house was only built in the early seventeenth century, so the poet was probably misled by the lady who made her living telling tall tales about the house. Sir Walter Scott chose this building as the fictional home of Catharine Glover in his novel The Fair Maid of Perth, which mixes real and imagined events and characters during the reign of King Robert III (1390–1406).

The Beautiful City of Perth

Beautiful Ancient City of Perth,
One of the grandest on the earth,
With your stately mansions and streets so clean,
And situated between two Inches green,
Which are most magnificent to be seen.

The North Inch is beautiful to behold,
Where the daisies and butter-cups their petals unfold,
In the warm summer time of the year,
While the clear silvery Tay rolls by quite near,
And such a scene will your spirits cheer.

The South Inch is lovely, be it said,
And a splendid spot for military parade,
While along the highway there are some big trees,
Where the soldiers can rest or stand at ease,
Whichever way their commanders please.

The surrounding woodland scenery is very grand,
It cannot be surpassed in fair Scotland,
Especially the elegant Palace of Scone, in history renowned,
Where some of Scotland's kings were crowned.

And the Fair Maid of Perth's house is worthy to be seen,
Which is well worth visiting by Duke, Lord or Queen;
The Fair Maid of Perth caused the battle on the North Inch
'Twixt the Clans Chattan and Kay, and neither
        of them did flinch,
Until they were cut up inch by inch.

The scenery is lovely in the month of June,
When trees and flowers are in full bloom,
Especially near by the Palace of Scone,
Where the blackbird is heard whistling all day
While near by rolls on the clear silvery Tay.

Of all the cities in Scotland, beautiful Perth for me,
For it is the most elegant city that ever I did see,
With its beautiful woodland scenery along the river Tay,
Which would make the tourist's heart feel gay,
While fishing for trout on a fine summer day.

There, the angler, if he likes to resort
For a few day's fishing, can have excellent sport,
And while he is fishing during the day,
He will feel delighted with the scenery along the river Tay,
And the fish he catches will drive dull care away,
And his toil will be rewarded for the fatigues of the day.

Beautiful city of Perth, magnificent to be seen,
With your grand statues and Inches green,
And your lovely maidens fair and gay,
Which, in conclusion, I will venture to say,
You cannot be surpassed at the present day.

1896   **The Reverend H. Armstrong Hall**

Writing about Sir John Everett Millais*
in *The Daily Graphic*, August 14, 1896

MILLAIS' LIFE AND WORK in Scotland were both closely
connected with and influenced by a city and a river. The city was Perth,

in the outskirts of which is situated Bowerswell House, the loved home of his wife's family, and with the immediate neighbourhood of which were linked many of the most intimate associations of the last forty years of his life. The river was the Tay, which, seen as the artist and the fisherman see it, rarely fails to appeal to the heart and the imagination. The Englishman who knows nothing of Perth beyond its comfortable hotel and its spacious and often bewildering railway station, is not seldom at a loss to understand the claim of the city to its title of 'fair'; but those who have lived there, as Millais did, can neither be blind to, nor fail to appreciate, the glories of its surroundings – the rolling Strath of Tay, the lavishly tinted and ever-changing woods, the distant hills, now purple with heather, now white with ice and snow, the majestic river, instinct with movement and life and sound.

'This is much better than the Riviera,' Millais said as he gazed away to the north from Perth Bridge one bright winter morning of last year. The climate too, suited Millais. 'I can't see to paint in London in November,' he used to say. 'But the winter in Perth is usually open, and while the days are sadly short, their brightness is a revelation to most Southerners wintering there for the first time.' It was not, therefore, to be wondered at that the President preferred to see the New Year in before returning to London.

And while atmospheric conditions and happy family associations link the President to the city of Perth, it was the spirit of the Tay which syren-like drew him to its banks and waters by a fascination which he found irresistible, and compelled him, as no other artist of his capacity had ever been compelled, to hasten to interpret its message and its song. Nor was the hold thus exercised likely to be weakened by the boundless facilities for sport provided by the river and its guardian woods. For he was a sportsman of the best type.

Yes, this 'message and its song' were ever in his heart; even in the long weary weeks of April and May, 1896, when his life was slowly ebbing away.

Sir John Everett Millais (1829–1896), artist and President of the Royal Academy. Millais was married to Euphemia Gray of Bowerswell House.

c.1899 **Alexander McLeish**

Songs of St Johnston

Address to the 'Fair City'
(Viewing it from an Elevated Spot in the Vicinity)

Where might we find a fairer scene than this?
That stretches now before us broad and wide:
The river sweeping on in stateliness,
Old Bertha rising on its verdant side;
Whilst wood and meadow, interspersed between,
Lend light and colour to the gorgeous scene.

Thy wondrous beauties charm'd the sons of Rome,
In those dark days when they o'erran the world;
Amid thy bosky haunts they made a home,
And there in vaunting pride their flag unfurl'd.
But, ah, they little reck'd how true – how brave
Were they whom they were seeking to enslave.

From every glen, from every rural vale,
The northern clansmen muster'd in their might;
Bold youths and warriors bow'd by many a gale
Alike were there – all eager for the fight.
High were the hopes that stirred that patriot band:
Better than life they loved their native land!

Resistless as the fiery darts of heaven,
Our gallant forbears on their foemen fell;
Nor did they pause until, all rent and riven,
They drove them from the land they loved so well.
But, ah! full many a true and noble life
Was sacrificed in that unequal strife.

'Twas thus our fathers broke Rome's boasted might!
'Twas thus a pagan race their freedom won!
'Twas thus they stood for liberty and right,
As through succeeding years their sons have done.
For while yon rugged mountains cleave the sky,
So long shall Scots in freedom live and die!

A foremost part, dear City! thou hast played,
On history's page thy dear name is renowned;
For 'twas within thy strong protecting shade
That the proud rulers of our land were crowned.
Thou wert, fair City, in that distant day,
The home of courtly pomp and pageantry.

Methinks I see thee, Bertha, as ye stood
When thou wert called our country's capital;
I see full many a mansion, quaint and rude,
Within the shelter of thy massive wall.
And flowing round about thee, dark and deep,
I see the moat – the guardian of thy sleep!

Well art thou worthy of that tender name,
Which loving lips hath fondly given to thee;
Well art thou worthy of thy wide-spread fame,
Well hast thou earned thy prosperity!

Long may thy sons strive after honest praise,
As their ancestors did in days bygone!
Long may thy daughters walk in virtue's ways;
May care and sadness be to them unknown!

Auld Craigie Knowes

There's a dear weel kent spot no far frae oor toon,
An' dear has it aye been to me,
For there in the sweet sunny springtime o' life
I hae wander'd and played fu' o' glee;
An' altho' I should roam far across the braid faem,
Far awa' frae its haughs an' its howes,
O fondly I'll cherish, while life still remains,
The mem'ry o' auld Craigie Knowes.

Chorus
I've heard fouk speak o' sunny lands
That lie ayont the sea,
I've heard them brag o' splendours
That are dazzlin' to the e'e;
But the dearest, fairest scene
In a' the world to me,
Is the bonnie, bonnie Knowes o' Craigie.

The laverock ascends wi' the dew on its breast,
To welcome the dawn o' the morn,
An' the sang o' the thrush frae yon blackthorn tree
Awa' on the saft wind is born.
An' the dew glitters bricht 'neath the sun's gowden beam
Where the kye an' the sheep calmly browse.

Sweet thoughts o' my childhood endear ilka scene
Thar lies roon' my auld Craigie Knowes.

I've watched the red sun as it sank in the west,
Far ahint yon wild mountains sae grey;
I've watched it be-gilding Kinnoull's sombre crest,
An' kissin' the breist o' the Tay.
An' I've pu'd the wild rose frae yon love haunted side,
Whaur in richest profusion it grows;
It was there someone whispered her promise to me,
On the green slopes o' auld Craigie Knowes.

The North Inch

A level stretch of unbroken green,
Girt round by many a fair and noble tree,
Where, sever'd from the city's busy scene,
We taste of nature's own tranquility.

There, when the summer flow'rs are fresh and sweet,
The young engage in many a jovial game;
There, too, the old are oftimes wont to meet,
And fight their youthful battles o'er again..

And kissing with his lips each blooming side,
Old kingly Tay goes gaily romping by;
Reflecting in its clear, pellucid tide
The changing glories of the summer sky.

And far away, half merging with the blue,
Yon lofty hills in rugged grandeur rise;

Methinks, when kiss'd by sunset's crimson hue,
No fairer scene is view'd by mortal eyes.

Barnhill

Aflame with glory, all the distant west
Reflects the splendours of the setting sun;
And on the gleaming river' placid breast,
Slow mingling with the waters as they run,
I see the clouds that o'er the heavens stray,
Fair fringed with many a colour bright and gay,
And, rising from the river's verdant side,
Old Barnhill her ample sides display,
Entrancing as a young and blushing bride
In all the pomp of bridal finery.
And, hark! from out yon stately elm near by
The joyous blackbird trills its evening lay,
Full oft, dear bird, at close of busy day
Thy song hath helped to chase life's cares away.

And mark how green yon orchard monarchs stand,
Their broad plumes waving softly to and fro,
With scented summer blossom all aglow;
So fair, it seems as though some elfin hand
Had hung each bough with wreaths of virgin snow;
When mellow autumn, beauteous and fair,
Dipped all the woodlands in her varied dyes,
How often have I gazed with envious eyes
Upon thy fruitful trees, sweet Barnhill,
And wonder'd if it were a grievous sin
To ope' thy orchard gates and enter in;

And there, unmindful of each hidden snare,
Taste of thy sweets so luscious and rare –
Ay, even though forbidden, eat my fill!

Oor Toon

A canty place is oor toon,
A couthy face has oor toon,
For lasses fair,
An' callants rare,
There's nane sae famed as oor toon.

The skies are blue roon' oor toon,
An' fair to view is oor toon,
Its birks an' bow'rs
Are fill'd wi' flow'rs,
Earth's paradise is oor toon!

An honour'd name has oor toon,
Enshrined in fame is oor toon,
In Scotia's fight
For truth an' right
The foremost aye was oor toon!

Gin ye should stray by oor toon,
Some orra day by oor toon,
Draw boldly near,
There's nocht to fear –
They're kindly fouk in oor toon.

Then here's to a' in oor toon,

Baith great an' sma' in oor toon!
May fortune show'r
Her richest dow'r
On ilka ane in oor toon!

* * *

THE
Twentieth Century

The Salutation Hotel

1901 **D. Brown Anderson**

Notes of a Rambler

IN SPITE OF SEVERAL close streets and foul closes, to which eye and nostril are willingly shut, there are certain broad ways containing noble buildings pleasing to the eye, satisfying to the aesthetic taste in this Fair City close to the lordly river, the very king of Scottish streams. The first walk of the visitor through the city of Perth is sadly disappointing; you must traverse it again and again before you see the Hospital founded by James VI, in 1587, the houses associated with the Fair Maid and Hal o' the Wynd, its churches, steeples, municipal buildings, libraries, banks, and shops – the ancient and modern in closer juxtaposition to each other than anything seen in Edinburgh – and begin to realise the charm of the place.

A leisurely patrol of the streets over, you wander out to the North Inch, where the citizens are recreating, the cattle browsing. Seated by the Tay, you glance over to Old Scone, and that broad do-main of the noble earl, sweeping in lordly pride over a vast territory; you cross the river to New Scone, the hill is ascended, and the valleys below revealed. A halt is made at the policies of Bonhard and Murrayshall, the horses slowly ascend onwards to the Carse, just at the pace enabling the eye to fasten on the rich harvest of scenic splendour that meets the gaze. The summit gained, off they trot, sniffing the mountain breeze, only slackening again at the descent on the tower of Balthayock, that ivy–clad adjunct of a fine mansion, so elevated in site as to command the sweep of the Carse immediately below. On you drive in this now sequestered road round by Glencarse House to that delicious wayside inn where many a man and horse pauses to slacken. Refreshed by the process, you bowl along at the foot of the hill of Kinnoull, midway between the lordly Kinfauns, the umbrageous Seggieden and the suburban Barnhill.

Faithful in memory to the author of *The Fair Maid of Perth*, the town has its Scott Street, while the poet's statue with his attached hound 'Maida' adorns the northern margin of the South Inch, all of which are seen in perfection in the leafy month, yet milk-white with 'may.' View it with us in the mild freshness of the morn, when citizens and visitors pass each other on the glorious green beneath the blue vault of heaven, vocal with the music of many birds that after much skimming through the air, cool their plumage in the waters of the Tay, wherein four-footed animals are now splashing their heels. Not the least loved of the many places in which we have wandered, this splendid South Inch of Perth must be commemorated in better words that we can apply to it.

1909   A. R. Hope Moncrieff

The Heart of Scotland

PERTH HAS HAD THE SOLDIERS of many armies quartered upon it, including Cromwell's troopers, and the Hessians encamped for long on the Inch after the Rebellion of '45. At that time barracks were so deficient that Cumberland's men had to be lodged in the parish church and meeting-houses, turned into dormitories by deal boards laid across the pews. Later on, soldiers would be billeted upon the townsfolk, as the militiamen were in my recollection; and their pay was so poor that they did not always prove honest guests. Gowrie House, presented by the loyal townsfolk to the victor of Culloden, was made into an Artillery Barrack, but afterwards given back to the town to serve as its jail and county buildings in exchange for ground above the South Inch, where the General Prison came to be built. This was originally a depot for French prisoners of war, the first batch of whom, confined in a church on their way from Dundee, stole all the brass nails, green baize, and other fittings they could lay hands on. The prisoners became increased to thousands, who on the whole have behaved better, for they are said to have been missed at the peace, having, indeed, spent in the city a good deal of money which they earned in part by ingenious industries. These foreigners appear as the unexpected means of importing cricket into Scotland, first played on the Inches of Perth by the English regiments sent to guard the depot.

English soldiers, one supposes, are not now needed to guard Perth, its ordinary garrison a small body of the Black Watch or other local regiment. Gone, too, are the militia whom I once came upon drawn up at the top of the 'Whins' without a stitch of uniform on, stripped to bathe by word of command. Military displays on the Inch will be less common than games of golf, cricket, and football, the last in its more unsophisticated forms, since this public space does not lend itself to the collection of gate-money; but the barefoot laddies who here kick about the 'leather' for their own divert, are the buds of those professionals that bloom out to such applause in the English enclosures. And the rules of football have changed even since my youth, when a band of youngsters from various public schools, gathered on the Inch for a Christmas game, found themselves all at loggerheads in an anarchy not yet divided into the kingdoms of 'Rugger' and 'Soccer.' Still more has the game been refined since a day when country folk coming down to market, about two miles out of Perth, met a man charging along the Crieff road, chased by a party of the Forty-Second with their kilts streaming in the wind; at first sight the fugitive was taken for a deserter, and the farmers drew aside to give him a fair chance, but it was only a Methven lad carrying off the ball from a match on the North Inch, nor could he be tackled till it was goaled in his house, half a dozen miles from the field. Scone had once a name for rough matches, at which limbs were often broken, but, as the proverb went, 'A's fair at the ba' of Scone.

* * *

1910–14 **Dr Bill Harding**

On Flows the Tay: Perth and the First World War

PERTH, HEMMED IN on the banks of the Tay, is bounded to the north and south by wide-open spaces called Inches. In 1910 there was an almost rural quality about the town. Street-traders, many of them children, were everywhere hawking their wares while the pony and trap competed with dogcarts in some of the narrow lanes. There were many horses, either diminutive ponies pulling small vans or massive stallions drawing heavy carts, and, of course, horse-drinking troughs at every corner. Then there were blacksmiths such as J. Ewart in the Newrow and carriage-hirers, J. Masterton for instance, in Mill Street. Sheep and pigs were daily driven through the streets to the killing-house, while bull and stallion parades were weekly events. Little Dunning Market, a medieval fair, still survived and every October it flooded the High Street with stalls to the noisy delight of gipsy hawkers and packs of dogs. Poaching was the most common crime and the Town council's greatest worry was anthrax. Sadly, there were still no ladies' lavatories and ice-cream shops were only just losing their 'dens-of-iniquity' image. But change was coming. Trams trundled through the city pursued by clouds of cyclists and there were even a few motorcars and motorbikes. In stark contrast to its rural nature, the city had the huge North British Dye Works run by the Pullar family, who had dominated Perth, socially and politically, for the last fifty years. No other factory or industry could match their power and wealth and the 2000 workers seemed secure and content. Perth was a city with a placid flavour, more Victorian than Edwardian.

The city's contentment was reflected in the pastimes and amusements based on the river and the Inches. Rowing clubs, some dating back to 1892, were maintained by local firms, and regattas, 'jolly boat races', were especially popular. Water carnivals were used to highlight national events, and angling clubs, using tackle bought from D. B. Crockart in County Place, were widely patronised. Courting couples hired rowboats in the summer evenings from D. Malloch or G. Dutch, while macho-stalwarts from the local swimming clubs exhibited their strength in the annual Perth-to-Dundee Swim. After all, a lady had swum it in 1906! Cricket was Perth's game. The County Cricket Club had recently done well against the West Indies and members were proud of their new Cricket Pavilion. Golf, another speciality, could be played at the Artisan Golf Club on the North Inch, the King James VI Golf Club on Moncrieff Island and the recently opened Craigie Golf Course. With Joe Anderson as the local star the city had won fame.

There were specifically working-class amusements, especially football, which had increased in popularity since the formation of the Perthshire Football League in 1884. Football could inspire great passion as was the case when St Johnstone Football Club were criticised, or enormous enthusiasm when they defeated Leith Athletic 4–3 in 1914. Gymnastic competitions, wrestling and boxing were all popular with the dye-workers, especially the latter, because of Perth's boxing champion, J. B. McNeil. Pigeon racing and beekeeping were rather specialised, while the allotments of the Working Men's Garden Association on Moncreiff Island attracted the retired worker. Billiards and dominoes were not considered 'respectable' despite the fact that both had leagues and the Carlton Billiards Room in South Street was rather splendid.

Middle-class pastimes were more cultured. Recitals were held in St John's Kirk. There was the Perth Musical Society as well as amateur theatricals, bazaars, fetes or 'the Berlioz method of learning French'. There were 'serious plays' at the Theatre. There was a Perth Whist Club, and dining out at the New Royal George Restaurant had become fashionable. For the young there were Tango Tea dances with the daring Tango, New Boston or Rag.

Some problems, of course, never change. Throughout the 19th

century, drink was the root of the social malaise in Perth and it had barely improved by 1910. There were ninety-five registered drinking howffs in the city and drink was cheap by any standard. It was even possible to buy two bottles of whisky and two of port for a mere 10s 6d from Matthew Gloag's Wine and Spirit Merchants, Kinnoull Street. The pubs in the centre of the city: Old Ship Inn; Stormont Arms; Britannia Inn; Glencoe; Empire and Bee Bar were ghastly drinking dens, each with a long history of drunken violence. Statistics show that 73% of all crime in 1910–1914 was drink-related and that drunken females were the greatest problem for the police.

Another side of the coin was immorality. In 1913, Perth had at least twenty-four full-time prostitutes, while prostitution at the time was listed as 'an occupation'. So sordid was the seamy side of Perth nightlife that the Town Council hired night patrols for the parks.

1929 Peter Baxter

Revelry

OLD-TIME SCOTTISH SEASONS lent themselves to occasions of boisterous revelry. High spirited youths donned fantastic garments – they disguised themselves – and paraded the streets of our cities; the hilarity gave pleasure to the producers and to those who witnessed it. Thus we get disguise, disguised: to 'guise, guisar, and the variant, guizzars. Some Scottish towns had adult, and some youthful guisars – others had none. Perth has been one of the 'ayes' in regard to the custom from time immemorial, and it continues till the present time. On Auld Year's Nicht the custom takes on an annual renewed life and activity in Perth.

One thing is necessary for a successful Hogmanay Night in Perth – good weather! One's memory fails to number the bad ones. The guisars issue forth and gather their harvest! What of the drawings?

Here we must do a little eaves-dropping. After two or three hours' 'turn', the groups meet under lamp-posts and count the spoil! The bigger boys arrogantly ask their smaller fellows – 'Here, you wee punchers, how much hae ye made?' 'Eichteen pence,' is the proud reply. Among the bigger boys (and girls) better results have accrued – from two or three shillings up. For a party of two or three this gives – a sixpence to spend, sixpence for the 'Pictures', and a sixpence to put in the school bank. Mother does not charge anything for face-washing soap!

1929 H. V. Morton

In Search of Scotland

PERTH, LIKE GLOUCESTER, where matches are made – this is no pun – is full of small, pretty girls. They spend the day, I am told, in dyeing the garments of Great Britain; but they appear to have nothing to do in the evening but to walk arm in arm up and down High Street until at some mysterious hour of the night they remember their homes and vanish.

I was told that I would not like Perth; but I never pay attention to such prophecies. I found Perth full of atmosphere. I was astonished to learn that Dr Macfarlane, in his famous *Tour*, considered Perth to be pervaded by 'the cheerful air of a provincial town in England'. This is, to me, incomprehensible. the air is cheerful enough, but it is as Scottish as a plate of cocky-leekie or a warm bannock.

The winds of the Highlands blow into Perth day and night. And the voice of 'Pairth' is the voice of Scotland! Here you meet memories of the clans for the first time. As soon as the stranger begins talking about Perth he is told how the Clan Chattan and the Clan Quhele fought thirty champions a side on the North Inch. Perth like an English provincial town? You might as well put a Highlander in gaiters and call him a Devonshire yokel!

Never for one minute can you feel unconscious of the wildness which lies beyond the gates of Perth: the roads go north to Pitlochry and Drumochter, to Blairgowrie, and to the Spittal of Glenshee; and at night, as you walk through grey stone streets, modern but still, in their sky-line and their grim bulk, recalling a more ancient Perth, you smell a wind that comes sweet over miles of desolate heather.

The River Tay, which the legions of Agricola hailed as the Tiber, gives a rare beauty to Perth as it runs swiftly beneath its bridges.

All cities which have played a great part in history retain, no matter how time alters them, an air of assurance and solidity, and this Perth possesses to an unusual degree. It is interesting to prowl round in search of Old Perth. You find, for instance, that the site of the still mysterious Gowrie Conspiracy is today the fine modern County Building.

Nothing could look less mysterious today than the site of Gowrie House; but that is the way with Perth. Like Dundee, it has turned its historic places to useful ends. Somewhere beneath Perth, I believe, sleep a king and queen. James I and his queen were buried in a Carthusian monastery on a site between the Hospital and King Street. If we could X-ray that ground perhaps we should find them there sleeping still with the glory and the woes of old Scotland still about them.

Perth deserves the gratitude of every man interested in architecture. This city has broken with the old-time Calvinism and has restored its splendid church of St John to something resembling its former glory. This excellent resurrection is Perth's War Memorial. I do not know what the sterner Presbyterians of the last generation would have said to all this. The services of the Church of Scotland are now held in one of the finest cathedrals in the country. St John's – like many another Scottish church – until recently housed three separate congregations! Now that the barriers are down it is possible to see for the first time for centuries its real beauty and the true proportions.

If Perth works hard at its factories, its railways, its cattle markets, it also plays hard. The city is the 'birthplace of cricket' in Scotland. A local antiquary told me an interesting story about this. 'During the Napoleonic wars,' he said. 'Perth housed thousands of French prisoners. They were guarded with great care, and several regiments of militia and one regiment of English cavalry were sent from the south. The Hussars played cricket on the South Inch – watched, of course, by the boyhood of Perth. So the game took root here, and has been played ever since. By the way, you may not know that during the first fifty years of its existence the Perth Cricket Club beat the famous I Zingari by thirteen runs...'

Perth, too, has made golf history. The game of golf dates its popularity from the invention of gunpowder. It was put down by law in the early days because Scotsmen practiced golf instead of archery, with the result that the English long-bow worked havoc among the ill-trained Scots archers. When gunpowder made bows and arrows obsolete, there was no longer any reason to prohibit golf, and the early clubs were made by the 'bowyers', who found their trade in bows declining. These clubs were made in Perth. In the old days Perth rivalled St Andrews as a golfing centre, and among its famous golfers was Bob Andrews, who could drive a ball off the face of a gold watch without damaging it!

I climbed Kinnoul Hill before breakfast. The morning was cold with the chill of early autumn, but the sun shone in a cloudless sky. When I left the road to strike up over grass to the summit my foot-steps were printed black behind me in the thick dewfall …

I have written of the views from high places in Edinburgh, Stirling and Dundee. What can I say of the country that spreads itself below Kinnoul Hill in the still hush of an autumn morning? It must be one of the grandest sights in all Scotland.

Perth and its clustered streets lie below – a 'fair city' on the banks of the Tay; and you follow the silver ribbon of water through the green Carse of Gowrie, watch it twisting through the fields, disappearing for a little while into woodland, then going on, widening mile after mile seaward between the shores of Forfar and Fife.

You have the impression that you are in a stationary airship. You are actually 729 feet above the plain. All the land lies crystal clear below you to the horizon, where the mountains lift their heads in a faint blue haze: nearer now, no longer vague peaks and ridges riding the sky as they seemed from the ramparts of Stirling Castle. There is a view indicator on the summit of Kinnoul Hill – a large disc covered by glass and protected by wire-netting – on which black arrows point over fifty miles of space to the distant peaks of the Grampians. The dew had fallen on it, covering the glass with drops of water, so that I had to take a stick and push a handkerchief under the wire to clean the glass before I could find my way over the rising and falling barrier of blueness that closed the tremendous view.

There can be no grander introduction to the Highlands of Scotland than to stand on Kinnoul Hill in the early morning and read the titles of the Grampians as you follow the flight of the black arrows – Ben-y-Gloe, Beinn Dearg, Cairn Toul, Ben Macdhui – and can that remote monster lurking in the misty distance be Ben Nevis?

On the way down I heard a school-bell ringing. Small boys with marvellous Scots faces were trying not to be early and not to be late. Their boots were polished as if for some competition. One of them came up to me. He was a typical young Scot, red, freckled, and blunt.

'Have ye a cigarette car-r-ud?'

I went through my pockets while he waited in a condition of suspended hope. I found him some.

'Who cleans your boots?'

'Masel'.'

'Do you like school?'

'I like it fine.'

'What are you going to be when you grow up?'

'I havena decided,' he replied with great gravity, 'but I'm

minded to be a farmer.'

What a refreshing lad! No engines in his soul!

He went whistling down the road, kicking the dew about with his polished boots until he met a friend, and from the look of the meeting I think that, like a true Scot, he was trading my cigarette cards for something he wanted more!

1930   **Hamish Miles**

Fair Perthshire

I HAVE MADE very small acquaintance with Perth itself. Chance has made me there only a transient visitor; and if I were to venture on purely personal knowledge of the city, the picture might be too fragmentary to please either the learned resident or the enquiring traveller. For it seems to centre, somehow, on the fascinating platforms of the General Station; there is the business of getting luggage down from the racks, glimpses of prisons, dyeworks, distilleries, the cries of the porters with the long-drawn vowel of 'Pe-e-erth,' the majestic bearing of the station-master, so long frock-coated and top-hatted and buttonholed, the large important clock, the baskets of game, and a fresh keenness even in the wind blowing down the sloping roadway up into town.... Or again, at other seasons, there might be memories of a very late supper of cold grouse at the Station Hotel, a very hot rum punch at the Salutation, recollections of stamping feet in trains waiting to start after a day of lamb-sales, and long, detailed discussions of prices – of why cross and half-breds had dropped this month, of stots and stirks keeping up their prices, lambs off the Mains of Mause at 44/9, Glendelvine 40/-, Ford of Pitcur, 36/-, Balquhandy Hill, 41/–.

* * *

c.1930 **A. A. Thomson**

Let's See The Highlands

BY A WINDING meadow-fringed road we came at last to Perth with the feeling that some, at least, of the best wine had been kept to the last. The Fair City of St. John is the usual gateway to the Highlands for those travellers who take the eastern road. Others, who, like ourselves, enter by the west, employ Perth's gateway as a final exit, but, going or coming, the gateway is in every way worthy of the land it guards.

Serene in beautiful old age, it sits upon the green bank of the Tay, flanked by its Inches – wide strips of level meadow, open to sky and river. Now on the North Inch you will see cricket matches played where once was fought one of the most thrilling fights in history, or fiction, when the thirty chosen champions of Clan Chattan and Clan Quhele did battle until almost all were slain.

1932 **A. R. Hope Moncrieff**

Scotland – the Fair City

PERTH, the central city of Scotland, whose name has been so flourishingly transplanted to the antipodes, is a very ancient place. Not to insist on fond derivation from a Roman Bertha, there seems to have been a Roman station on the Tay, probably at the confluence of the Almond; and curious antiquarians have found cause for confessing to Pontius Pilate as perhaps born in the county, a reproach softened by the consideration of his father being little better than a Roman exciseman. The alias of St Johnston, Perth got from its patron saint who came to be so scurvily handled at the Reformation. At this date it was the only walled city of Scotland. Before this, it had been intermittently the Stuart capital in such a sense as the residence of its Negus is

for Abyssinia; and further back Tayside was the seat of the Alpine kingdom that succeeded a Pictish power. Now sunk in relative importance,
Perth makes the central knot of Scottish railway travelling; so on the
Eve of St. Grouse its palatial station becomes one of the busiest spots
in the kingdom, though the main platform is a third of a mile long. To
the stay-at-home public it may perhaps be best known by an industry
that has given rise to the proverb 'See Perth and dye,' one which might
have darker significance in days when this low site depended for
drainage on the floods of the Tay flushing its cellars and cesspools. But
its own citizens are brought up to believe that no Naples of them all
has so much right to the title of the 'Fair City'.

Legend tells how Roman soldiers gaining a prospect of the
Tay from the heights south of Perth, exclaimed on its North Inch as
another Campus Martius; but later visitors have not always shared the
local admiration. One modern Italian traveller, Signor Piovanelli, after
wandering two or three hours about the Perth streets, took away an
impression of dull melancholy; but then he began with an unsatisfac-
tory experience at the Refreshment Room. An early conscientious
French tourist explains the bustle of Perth station as its being the
rendezvous of the inhabitants seeking distraction from their *triste* life.
These be ignorant calumnies. At least our northern York is a typical
Scottish town, well displaying the strata of its development. In quite
recent years it has been much transmogrified by a new thoroughfare,
fittingly named Scott Street, which, running from near the station right
through the city, has altered its centre of gravity. The old High Street
and South Street, with their 'vennels' and 'closes,' lead transversely
from Scott Street to the river, cut at the other end by George Street and
John Street which had supplanted them as main lines of business.
'Where are the shops?' I was once asked by a party of country excur-
sionists, wandering unedified about the vicinity of the station. In those
days one had to send them across the city to the streets parallel with
the river; but now Scott Street has attracted the Post Office, the

Theatre, and the Free Library, and bids fair to become the Strand or Regent Street of the Fair City.

From the windings of the Blackfriars quarter, one emerges by what was the North Port, upon Perth's famous Inch, bordered by erections that a generation ago were the modest West End of the city – Athole Place, the Crescent, Rose Terrace and Barossa Place. At the foot of the Inch, by the river, stands a tall obelisk in honour of the 90th Regiment, 'The Perthshire Volunteers,' now amalgamated with the Cameronians; and near it the customary statue of Prince Albert, one of the first inaugurated by Queen Victoria, who then insisted on knighting the Lord Provost of the city, a worth grocer, much to his discontent, and, if all tales be true, to his loss in business. Perth, as becomes the ex-capital, has a Lord Provost, who cannot meet the Lord Provost of Glasgow without raising sore points of precedence.

By the bridge at the foot of the North Inch, a pretentious classical structure, marking the era of Provost Marshall whom it commemorates, rears its dome above a Museum of Antiquities such as becomes an ancient city. This faces the end of Tay Street, the pleasant river-side boulevard between the North and South Inches, towards the further end of which a newer Museum contains a remarkable natural history collection. At its corner of South Street are the County Buildings, adorned with portraits of local worthies, and at the end of High Street, the City Buildings with windows illustrating Perth's history. Perth has now two bridges and everything handsome about it – besides the Dundee railway bridge with its footway from the South Inch. The central bridge was constructed early in our century, but here stood one washed away in 1621, since when the citizens had long to depend on what is now the old bridge below the North Inch.

This bridge leads over into the transpontine suburb, above which, on the slopes of Kinnoul Hill, the rank and fashion of the city have inclined to seek 'eligible building sites,' Scottice, 'feuing plots.' The banks of the river, too, on this side have long been bordered by villas and terraces of gentility; but about 'Bridge End' there is still a fragment of the humbler suburb that has had more than one famous sojourner in our time. Here, in a house now distinguished by a tablet, and afterwards in Rose Terrace opposite, John Ruskin spent bits of his childhood with an aunt, wife of the tanner whose unsavoury business had the credit of keeping the cholera away from Bridge End. That amateur of beauty, for his part, has nothing but good to say of Perth: he remembers with pleasure the precipices of Kinnoul, the swirling pools of the 'Goddess-river', even the humble 'Lade' in which other less gifted children have found 'a treasure of flowing diamond,' now covered up to belie his vision of its defilement; and his life-long impression was that 'Scottish sheaves are more golden than are bound in other lands, and that no harvests elsewhere visible to human eyes are so like the 'corn of heaven' as those of Strath Tay and Strath Earn.'

Many a stranger comes and goes at Perth without guessing what charming prospects may be sought out on its environing heights. But half an hour's stroll through the streets must make him aware of those Inches that prompt a hoary jest concerning the size of the Fair City. The North and South Inches, between which it lies, properly islands, green flats beside the Tay, are in their humble way its Hyde Park and Regent's Park. The South Inch, close below the station, is the less extensive, once the grounds of a great Carthusian monastery, then site of a strong fort built by Cromwell, now notable mainly for the avenue through which the road from Edinburgh comes in over it, and for the wharf at its side that forms a port for small vessels and excursion steamers plying by leave of its tide. On the landward side, beyond the station, Perth is spreading itself up the broomy slopes of Craigie Hill, which still offers pleasant rambles. Beyond the further end stands a gloomy building once known to evil-doers as the General Prison for Scotland; but of late years its character has undergone some change; and I am not sure how far the old story may still keep its point that represents an inmate set loose from these walls, when hailed by a friendly wayfarer as 'honest man,' giving back glumly 'None of your dry remarks!'

Now let us take a dander up the larger North Inch, Perth's Campus Martius, at once promenade, race-course, review ground, grazing common, washing green, golf links, cricket-field, and area for unfenced football games in which, summer and winter, young Scots learn betimes to earn gate-money for English clubs. Opposite the Perth Academy appears to have been the arena where that early professional, Hal o' the Wynd, played up so well in the deadly match by which the Clan Kay and the Clan Chattan enacted the less authentic tragedy of the Kilkenny cats. This spacious playground is now edged by a neat walk, which makes the constitutional round of sedate citizens, who on the safe riverside have the spectacle of pleasure boating against the difficulties of a strong stream and shallow rapids, and of the pulling of salmon nets in the season. Here a bare-legged laddie, with the rudest tackle, has been known to hook a 30-lb. fish, holding on to the monster for two hours till some men helped him out with his fortune. The salmon of the Tay, reared in the Stormontfield Ponds above Perth, are famous for size, a weight of over 70 lbs. being not unknown. The keeping of fish in ice, and railway communications, have much enhanced the price, to the astonishment of a Highland laird who in a London tavern ordered a steak for himself and a 'salmon for Donald' without gussing that his henchman's meal must be paid for in gold as his own in silver. But so masterful are the demands of London now, that salmon may sometimes be dearer on the banks of the Tay than in the glutted metropolitan market. The Tay has another treasure, for now and then valuable pearls have been fished out of it by boys who, in a dry summer, can wade across its shallows just above the old bridge. A very different sight might be seen here when the river was frozen across and roughened by a jam of miniature icebergs.

Above the Inch comes the less trim space called the 'Whins,' where lucky caddies glean lost golf balls in its patches of scrub and in pools formed by the highest flowing of the tide from the Firth, With this ends the public pleasure-ground; but the walk may be prolonged along the elevated bank of the river, above the sward that makes the town bathing place. One deep swirl within a miniature promontory is aptly known as the 'Pen and Ink'; then higher up a shallow creek encloses the 'Woody Island,' no island to bare-legged laddies who here play Robinson Crusoe.

If any ill-advised stranger find the streets of the Fair City dull, as would hardly be his lot on market-day, let him turn to Kinnoul Hill for a noble scene, and to the Tay banks for a characteristic one of broad fields and stately woods, backed by the ridge of the Grampians a dozen miles away.

1932 **J. J. Bell**

The Glory of Scotland

THE NAME PERTH may be a corruption of Bertha, a trad - itional town, two miles up the river, which was washed out, along with its dwellers, by a great flood on the year 1210. At all events, Perth is very old, and was Scotland's capital before Stirling, which had the honour before Edinburgh. Today it is a modern, cheerful place of some 35,000 inhabitants, with a long history, though not very much to show for it.

We know that James VI was a golfer, and Perth likes to think that he played on the North Inch as well as at St Andrews. Perth does not, however, like to think that the North Inch course less abundantly merits the title 'Royal' than the course at Dornoch, in the far North, which received the title after King Edward VII had blandly viewed it from a distance. Anyway, it is pleasant to picture James – who would, no doubt, consider our plus-fours unfashionably long – following his ball of feathers with a stiff timber club over that magnificent stretch, now part of a fine public park.

There is a South Inch also, crossed by the Edinburgh road through an avenue of trees, its most prominent, though not most cheering, sight being the General Prison for Scotland, the oldest part of which was built for the confinement of French prisoners in Napoleon's day. The word inch here means 'island', and there was a time, as you may learn by examining the slopes above the banks of the Tay, when the river – or was it the sea? - flowed at a higher level than now. A water-surrounded inch remains in Moncrieffe Island, which carries a very delightful 18-hole course on splendid turf, three miles long, though all the hazards, owing to the flat ground are artificial. A newer course, with natural hazards, will be found on Craigie Hill, which, like the island course, is only about ten minutes' walk from the city. While near the river, let me tell the angler that he can have free fishing during the season for trout, and in the autumn for salmon, over a two-and-a-half miles stretch, from the top of the North Inch downward. As to other fishing waters, Mr P. D. Malloch, of 26 Scott Street, is always willing, I believe, to give information and expert advice. The river, too, is excellent for boating.

The Salutation Hotel, in South Street, was there when Prince Charlie came to Perth in 1746, and contains the room where he lay. Its spacious dining-room, with the great, high, arched window and musicians' gallery, is worth seeing.

Scone, is one of those funny words of ours which are so apt to bother the stranger. In the twelfth century it was written 'Scoone', and is still pronounced 'Skoon'. The scone of the tea-table is, however, pronounced 'skon', not 'skone'. You may care to remember this if, in the course of your tour, you should want to inquire whether they bake good scones at Scone.

* * *

1932–42 **William Soutar**

St. Johnstoun and Other Poems

St. Johnstoun

St. Johnstoun is a merry toun
Whaur the water rins sae schire;
And whaur the leafy hill looks doun
On steeple and on spire.

St. Johnstoun is a merry toun
At play-day or at work:
The water sings, the causey rings,
The bells cry frae the kirk.

And whan the carse is green and gowd,
And the water skimmers on,
Wha wudna be baith merry and proud
To bide in St. Johnstoun?

Yon Toun

Hae ye come in be yon toun
Ablow the Craigie Knowes?
Hae ye come in be yon toun
Whaur the clear water rows?

Birk and rodden on the brae,
Hawthorn in the hauch;
And clear water churlin by
The elder and the sauch.

At day-daw and at grey-fa'
The merry bells ding doun;
At day-daw and grey-fa'
There's music in yon toun.

Merle and mavie whistle clear;
And whan the hour is still
Haikers owre the auld brig hear
The gowk upon the hill.

Wha wudna bide in yon toun
Ablow the Craigie Knowes?
Wha wudna bide in yon toun
Whaur the clear water rows?

Thrang and Thrivin

Wha daunders round St Johnstoun,
Or up and doun onie gate,
Will gang by monie a kirk and pub,
And monie a doctor's plate.

But whether a rowth o' preachin
Is byord'nar drouthy wark;
Or whether a rowth o' leechin
Maks folk keep in wi' the kirk.

Or whether a rowth o' drinkin
Needs a rowth o' physic and prayer –
Ye winna be lang in thinkin
They're a' thrang and thrivin there.

Backlands

In backlands aff the Ropey Close,
When the mune grows cauld and sneep,
The bairnies wha were beddit boss
Hae grat themsel's to sleep.

The auld wife, boo'd abune her wark
Sleeks on be cannel-flame;
The sma'-hour dinnles through the dark;
The trollop taivers hame.

In St Johnstoun

At midnicht whan the wee bells dinnle
And syne the muckle bell
A' the dockers frae the Coo Vennel
Howder doun to the well.

On ilka nicht they haik the cundie
And owre the cobble-stanes;
But atween the Sabbath-day and Monday
They aye bide in their dens.

There isna onie body,
Nor the Lord Provost himsel',
Kens what gars them haud in sae hoddie;
Bur nae doot they ken themsel!

* * *

1933 **John Buchan**

From his Speech on being made a
Freeman of the City of Perth

I AM ONE OF YOURSELVES. ....My notion of Perth was drawn wholly from Sir Walter Scott, and it seemed to me a magical place which must confer a unique distinction upon its natives.

1934 **W. S. Percy**

Strolling Through Scotland

PERTH CAN TRULY be called the 'Gateway to the Highlands'. Rival clans fought out their savage feuds five centuries ago on the North Inch, where today concert parties have their pitch and youthful footballers practice and prepare for their acceptance by some future English team. And, while the Tay flows steadily and calmly under its many bridges, charabancs whirl you away for a day to the Rob Roy country, and land you back at night to sleep in the room where Bonnie Prince Charlie once slept.

Perth owes a lot to the late Lord Dewar, the finest after-dinner speaker of his day. Though centuries divide them I would like to have matched him with that bumptious old bounder of Fleet Street, Dr Samuel Johnson, who would be in the discard if it were not for his Scottish biographer.

The High Street is a busy modern street, but you have only to glance at the notices displayed on different houses to trace its history. One end of the street finishes abruptly at the Tay. Here once stood the old Perth Bridge which was destroyed by flood in 1621, and near here the Battle of the Brig was fought in 1547.

If you walk a few yards away, on your left you will notice a sign above a shop:

Site of the Town House
of the family of Mercer, Merchant
Princes of the 14th Century.

Subsequently there stood here the House of the Green, a famous hostelry and favourite resort of the county lairds. This house and its hostess are immortalised in a poem by Lady Nairne, entitled 'Kitty Reid's House'.

But this spot goes much further back. When the ground was excavated for laying the foundation of the present house, two apartments were discovered each twenty-six feet by fourteen feet with strongly cemented walls three and a half feet thick. This is supposed to have been a temple of the early Britons long before the Roman invasion, and the name of the old inn is said to have been taken from it.

A few yards away on the same side is the site of the house in which Mrs Kennedy-Fraser, the collector of 'The Songs of the Hebrides' was born. The tablet was erected by the Gaelic Society of Perth, but Mrs Kennedy-Fraser has erected her own monument by her great work, which will live for ever.

Close by, where now stands a hotel called the Parliament Bar, once stood the Parliament House, from whence Scotland was ruled.

Across the road, a small passageway leads to 'The Fair Maid's House'. Next to the Fair Maid's House is the site of the Town House, occupied from 1758 to 1798 by Lord John Murray, Governor of H. M. Forces. There are many fair maids in Perth still, and since that tiny, talented woman in Hollywood wrote *Gentlemen Prefer Blondes*, some of them are even more fair.

A few yards away the Castle of Perth once stood, the original of which also has been ascribed to Agricola. The castle was the Perth residence of the Scottish Kings until the Blackfriars Monastery was erected.

In the Salutation Hotel you can see where Bonnie Prince

Charlie slept. Let us hope he slept peacefully – he probably needed it. Poor young man!

The railway station of Perth, like many other stations in Scotland, stands on historic ground, for here was once the Priory Hospital and Chapel of St Leonards, which was suppressed in 1434. The names of the streets surrounding it still bear traces of the old hospital, St Leonards Bank and Bridge, Abbot Street and Priory Place.

The new Art Gallery has done away with a lot of slum buildings. This building is a case where the architect has planned to glorify one of the most elegant buildings in Perth. It was erected to commemorate the public services of Provost Marshall. It is circular in form and has an Ionic portico surmounted by a dome, now part of the new buildings, and the dignity of the old and the modern spirit of the new are happily wedded.

Canal Street gets its name from the moat that once ran round the town. When Bruce captured the town, he filled up this ditch, and its only indication is the name of the street.

Perth is without doubt one of the prettiest towns in Scotland, borrowing much of its beauty from the broad current of the Tay moving majestically past, and from its two vast expanses of public meadows. Except from the east it is surrounded by hills that enclose it like an amphitheatre; the prospects from Kinnoull and from High Craigie are both beautiful. No wonder the Romans, when they marched over Baiglie, exclaimed, 'Behold the Tiber!'

1935 **Campbell Nairne**

Scottish Country

FOR ME the core of the universe was Perth. A Mr Willis who took coach through our barbaric land about the end of the eighteenth century paused for a moment in his appraisal of 'gentlemen's seats' to remark that Perth is the most elegantly built of any town in Scotland, and that 'the light and beautiful bridge which throws itself like a rainbow over the Tay is deservedly admired.' Lord Cockburn, who joggled from Edinburgh a few decades later to hold court in Perth, wrote of it as 'this rose of country towns' - a compliment inspired, one fancies, by the smooth workings of his Lordship's digestion, for there is evidence that we dined him well.

Ignorant of these tributes, but already a stout local patriot, I used to conclude essays with the pronouncement that Perth is rightly known as the Fair City. It is the strangest of titles. By 'city' we do not usually understand a town which has fewer inhabitants than a metropolitan housing scheme – I mean one of these red bungaloid rashes which it pleases the perpetrators to call garden suburbs. And 'fair' is not perhaps a just epithet now that we can boast of a disproportionately-sized railway station, a slum or two, and even, here and there, a hulk of windowless factory, with a stalk dribbling smoke towards the steep of Kinnoull Hill.

On the other hand there is still a bleating of sheep across the road from Dewar's red-brick warehouses, the collies go 'way wide' under the panache of smoke thrown up by the London express, red-faced men in tweeds climb down stiffly out of the brakes and gigs that come *clip-clop clip-clop* into town on market days behind the swift-sliding motor-cars, and Lord Cockburn's perfumed phrase is not yet without meaning. It may actually reacquire its old aptness. In recent years the octopus of industrialism has begun to drop back from Perth, and it looks as though we shall soon be left with nothing but its putrescent tentacle about our vitals.

* * *

1935 **William Roughead**

'Death In Cuddies Strip' (from *Mainly Murder*)

...THERE IS A FALSE but widespread and persistent rumour that this young girl of seventeen, when she left home that evening for a three-hours' walk with her lover, had on no stitch of clothing other than her outer coat, that being, as is alleged, on such occasions a common practice among the modern Fair Maids of Perth! If it indeed be so, then their disregard of propriety is only equalled in effrontery by their defiance of the local climate.

1938 **A. K. Bell**

From his Speech on being made a
Freeman of the City of Perth

I HAVE BEEN TWICE across America, through a considerable part of Europe, and three times through Australia and New Zealand, and I have failed to find one spot which I would prefer to live in than our Fair City.

1939 **Lawrence Melville**

The Fair Land of Gowrie

LEAVING PERTH and crossing the Tay by the Old Bridge, our road is up the steep Lochy Brae. Recalling the pack horses and stage coaches which more than a century ago were the means of transport, we may well wonder why the road should start with a 'stey brae,' even although it is said that the river did at one time flow along the foothills of the Carse, some distance to the north of its present course. At the top of the brae, on our right, is Potter Hill House, one of the first mansions to be built on the Bridgend side of the Tay. The grounds contain many fine old trees, in which several colonies of rooks have nested for generations.

Further up on the right, a by-way leads to the old clachan or hamlet of Corsiehill, which possibly will have disappeared from off the map and the Valuation Roll, before we go to print. In 1936, the Perth County Council took steps for the evacuation of Corsiehill, lying on the slopes of Kinnoull Hill. Formerly it may have consisted of at least twenty cottages, but practically every house has been condemned by the Department of Health. The only residenters who will remain are the three owner-occupiers of cottages. The old houses are in ruins and the lack of any sort of water supply has precluded the possibility of a new community springing up on the site of the picturesque old village.

Before we leave Corsiehill we are reminded of Burns' journey through the Carse of Gowrie to Perth, which was by the 'high or braes road,' by Castle Huntly and Fingask. On arriving at Corsiehill there was the fine view of Scone Palace, of which Burns took note ere he crossed the Perth Bridge and entered Perth. Burns visit was of date 14th and 15th September, 1787.

1944-53 **David McCormack**

Memories of Perth

FIVE O'CLOCK – on a fine spring morning, in 1944. I stand at my bedroom window and gaze at the wealth of gorgeous blossom upon the boughs of the apple trees within the garden. A thrush glides down upon the lawn and awaits a morning tit-bit. A tit is pecking at a broken cocoanut. Dunsinane and Bole Hill, within the sun-lit lands of Rait, adorn the scene.

I cross the hall, and stepping into the front room, I look across the open field towards the bonnie knowes of Craigie. Along the green ridge of the hill the entrancing larch trees are wonderfully outlined against the brilliance of an opal coloured southern sky; the grassy slopes lie peacefully enshrined in the gleam of a cloudless dawn; the path to Greenfield, where it passes by the well of St Mary Magdalene, is prettily merged into the shadows of the firs.

Five o'clock – the summer sun is creeping up behind Kinnoull and decorating the Inch with dewdrops: five o'clock – the curlews are calling from the marshlands, and the cocks are crowing loudly from the farms. Five o'clock – the crows are fluttering round the tops of the elm trees, and the blackbird and the thrush are whistling in the boughs. Five o'clock – the world is awaking from its short repose and Tom Henderson is on his way to ring the early morning bells of St John's.

Five o'clock – nay! The half-hour bells have started in the steeple of St Paul's and it is time to go. Here is Farquharson the Chemist on his way to the icy cold river for a morning bath; there is Dunbar the Horse-dealer unlocking the door of his stables; here is smiling Nellie Melville journeying to Pullars'.

...The unattractive history of man, in contrast with the constant stillness and beauty of unending nature was first presented to my mind on the South Inch of Perth.

Along its many fine avenues of stately trees; in the shadowy precincts of the grey walls of the Penitentiary, on the rough, weed strewn banks of the wagon depot of the locomotive works; on the thin brown paths which crossed the meadow like cracks in a deep green plate; at the encircling seats of the massive trunks of the two great chest-nut trees on which effective storms have raged; on the cinder covered showground with its whin decorated gallery of Princes Street Railway Station; on the unfriendly banks of St Leonards, and around the plaintive sadness of the monument to Sir Walter Scott, nature never seemed to array herself in her best attire. The air, though fresh, lacked nimbleness; the grass, though green, lacked charm, and the lively sprites within the sunbeams were tired and clumsy when they danced.

It was not a lack of attractions that made the South Inch dull. Circuses, menageries, and all the fun and glitter of the fair were seldom absent from it. The South Inch is the show-ground of Perth. Those who remember the permanent building that housed Cooke's Circus may also visualize the happy water scene that brought each day's performance to its close. Like me, they may decide to stroll among the crowd and enjoy the merry clamour of the shows.

There, in the bright glare of the leaky burners of the long-tailed naphtha lamps, boys and girls, bubbling over with merriment, are tightly clinging to the large twisted rods of glowing burnished brass which support the now rapidly revolving framework of the bobbing hobby horses. Round and round they go to the brisk accompaniment of the thin blare of the tin trumpets of the highly decorated hurdy gurdy organ.

...The other evening, as I idly turned over the pages of *The Select London Stage*, I recalled those rather far-off days when I regularly skipped up the long, steep stair-case in the Cutlog Vennel to a seat in the gallery of the Perth Theatre. There, among what was sure to be a happy and jovial crowd, I sat amid the noise and bustle till the lights of the 'gods' were lowered and the lights of the stage went up. A veritable cushion of silence heralded the rise of the curtain. Late-comers, if any, must have then tip-toed very gently to their seats, for, I am sure, not a single spectator was ever in the least disturbed. Each heart was with the players and each mind dwelt within the pageantry of the play.

* * *

Craigie Knowes

Along the pleasant banks of Tay,
In many a livelong summer's day;
I've sung the ever tuneful lay
Of the bonnie knowes o' Craigie.

By Springland's ivy mantled tower
I've rowed to Annaty's fair bower,
As the gleam of twilight's peaceful hour
Crept o'er the knowes o' Craigie.

I've climbed he hill of Murrayshall,
As evening heard the blackbird's call,
And watched the moonlight softly fall
On the bonnie knowes o' Craigie.

Ere the blithe skylark stirred the corn,
I've trod Kinnoull at early morn,
To see the rising sun adorn
The bonnie knowes o' Craigie.

I've gaed through lonely Quarrymill,
Fair Lignwood's fields and Dowie's rill,
Quiet Gannochy and Lochy Hill,
To the bonnie knowes o' Craigie.

Let us again the toast declare,
Here's to Perth, the city fair,
The lads and a' the lassies there,
And the bonnie knowes o' Craigie.

1947 **Seton Gordon**

Highways and Byways in the Central Highlands

THE NORTH INCH of Perth is, after more than five centuries, still open grassy land on which no building is permitted. On the winter day when I visited that old historic battlefield the Tay was frozen across, and against the piers of the bridge spanning the stream the ice had been pressed high by the current. In the open 'lanes' of water a great assembly of waterfowl were feeding. The majority of the birds were mallard but it was more unexpected to see handsome golden-eye drakes swimming and diving in full view of the citizens of Perth. Herring gulls were standing disconsolately on the ice, and black-headed gulls – small gulls with pointed, black-tipped wings – were flying restlessly to and fro and, like their relations of the London parks, were taking food from the hands of their human friends.

The North Inch is now set aside for the purpose of peaceful recreation, but I do not imagine that the character of its ground has greatly changed since 1396, when its level, grassy acres must have formed an ideal setting for the sanguinary conflict watched by the King and his nobles and the citizens of Perth.

1950–1 **Dr James Morton**

The Dusty Road From Perth

1950

But the day I had been waiting for came near the end of my one-week stay in Edinburgh. It came with a strange mixture of longing and fear – longing to see Perth and fear that it could not possibly justify the image I had of it. 'I've written to Maymie Padkin,' Uncle John said, 'and we've to come up on the twentieth.' I had planned to go there alone – to walk anonymously along the streets that I already knew so well, to climb Kinnoull Hill, to run upon the North Inch, to lean on the fence of the Muirton and allow my sentimental soul to simmer and burst into a great mushrooming cloud of emotion. I had, I suppose, expected to experience a tremendous sensuous binge in Perth – and Uncle John was hardly the type with whom one could share such an emotional experience. He was kind and friendly but completely devoid of sentiment. But there was no escape. It was a minor disappointment. There was a bond between us and I could not expect to go alone.

Furthermore, he would be able to show me places I would have difficulty finding were I alone – and I could always go back.

But who was Maymie Padkin? Uncle John informed me that she was the daughter of Aunt Chrissie, one of the fourteen children born on the Muirton in the mid-nineteenth century. I remembered Aunt Chrissie. My father had mentioned her, though I did not know he had a cousin, Maymie Padkin Lindsay, living in the city.

September 20. Porridge and treacle and tea and the train – and Kinross, Dunfermline, Glenfarg and Bridge of Earn – and no one need tell me that this is the Tay and the tower on Kinnoull, that the stationmaster still wears a frock coat and a tile hat, as he did in my father's day. Here, though, is a modern bus, and it carries us up South Street, past Methven and John and George streets, which I know so well, and there is Prince Albert's Monument on the North Inch, and the bridge, and the Tay – where salmon run and pearls lie, according to my mother and my father.

The fact that it was a dull, cold day was of no consequence. I was at last in Perth, the home of my ancestors, my home – and every sight and sound stirred my soul – and essentially I was alone. Uncle John sat silently, stolidly beside me on the bus, staring straight ahead, his right leg stretched down the aisle, his hands resting on the cane which stood erect between his legs. To Uncle John it might as well have been Edinburgh or Philadelphia or Vancouver. It was an everyday trip on a bus to him. He did not know how I felt, though perhaps that is unfair. Behind his inscrutable mask, he might have sensed my emotion but chose not to broach the subject. My father would have reacted the same way, though he could not have hidden his own emotion. We walked up Muirhall Terrace to Gannochy Road – and there was the house where my father was born. Uncle John's cane pointed to the very window. A sign on the gate read Gannochyfold, and I remembered my father laboriously cutting letters from a sheet of aluminium and attaching them, with brass screws, to the gate that he had hung from the pillars at the foot of the driveway. 'It's not changed much.' Uncle John muttered. 'Only the lime trees have gone.' Did he not feel any emotion towards the house where he was raised and where his mother died just ten years earlier? I remembered when it happened and I can still see my father on his haunches, repairing the front steps as I awkwardly expressed my regrets to him. How did Uncle John feel that day? He would have been sad, but externally he would not have shown it. He would dust the tables and chairs and the mantel and eat at Binns, and his waitress and the old blether who was so stuck in his ways would not notice any difference in him from any other day. And he showed no emotion now as he turned and limped off down the hill to the Tay.

'This must be Lochy Brae, Uncle John.' I said, perhaps in a tone which he would reserve for such hallowed spots as the Shrine in the castle.

'Aye.' he answered through his pipe.

'And that must be where Miller, the baker, had his shop.'

'Aye.'

'And that's the Sawmill Stream?' I asked, now on the bridge.

'It is.'

He did not even seem surprised at my knowledge of the town.

'And where is Woody Island, Uncle John?'

'Around the bend a bit.' and he pointed upriver with his cane.

My father repaired his boat here and rowed my mother up the

river and tied up to that little float over there. The river is clear and brown and perhaps there are pearls amongst the stones.

'Could I see the North Church, Uncle John?'

'Och, we've nae time for that.'

'Could we go past Sharpe's School?'

'Och, we've nae time for that.'

Perhaps I resented his lack of understanding, but he could never destroy those precious moments when we hesitated on the bridge across the Tay with the North Inch – where my father played rugby in his youth and where my mother walked with Harry Murdoch and her sisters on a Sunday afternoon – stretching off to the distant borders of the Muirton.

Another bus carried us through the town to Cherry Hill and the Lindsays. It was just like a Scottish home in Burnaby; there was the same hominess and the same habits, the same expressions, the same food. My father's cousin, however, had something that was lacking in Uncle John and, to a lesser extent, in my father. She had a deep interest in the family and in the past, and she recognised the same in me. Immediately after lunch her husband, a great angular seed-potato farmer, appeared with a pencil and paper. 'I've to make a list of all the things you want to see in Perth,' he announced. I was afraid to look at Uncle John. 'Och, we've nae time for that,' he had said so often. He would be bored. He just liked to sit and blether.

Uncle John was correct to some extent. We had little time, but we drove about in David Lindsay's Austin and we saw Perth Academy and Sharpe's School. A sexton opened the doors of the North Church for us and I sat in the pew where my father's family had sat and I saw the choir where stern old Harry Murdoch had sung and kept an eye on his daughters. At the Muirton, the present tenant, Mr Clarke, welcomed us. 'Welcomed' is hardly correct. He tolerated us. He was a canny little man, pear shaped, sharp featured, with a cap on his head and trousers that clasped his ankles just above his boots. He stood with his hands inside his belt and looked somewhat askance at three members of the family of tenant farmers who had preceded him. But he pointed out the barns and byres where my father played as a child, and the old house, which Uncle David rebuilt because he believed it vibrated, and the Toll House on the Dunkeld Road and the little cottage where my father's Uncle John lived with his two sisters, Chattie and Lizzie.

It was late in the afternoon before we reached Wellshill. Here, Maymie said, was the family ground. On it stood a monument stretching high above all the rest. It had a square granite base and a long marble spire, but more remarkable were the inscriptions on three sides of the base. It recorded the deaths of every member of the family, in various corners of the world, from John in 1880 to David in 1937. It was all there before us on that cold September afternoon. Who were these strange ancestors – this John and his fourteen children, all born on the Muirton Farm? Some names were vaguely familiar. I had heard my father speak of his wealthy Uncle Andrew, but why, if he was the eldest child, had he forfeited his birthright to die in South Pasadena, which the stone stated was in 'Calafornia'? John, the second son – my father's Uncle John – I remembered as a bachelor living with his two sisters. And William, the third son, died in Calloa, Peru? I remembered my father telling us of an uncle who died in Peru after being bitten by a snake. Could he be the subject of this exciting tale from my childhood? And here was James, the sixth son, who died in 1891 when he was forty and his son, my father, was three years of age. Had he died three years earlier, the pillars would not have been built at the foot of the driveway and I would not have existed. It was all there before me, written in stone, on that dull, cold September day in 1950.

*   *   *

1951

The weather had kept me away from Perth, though perhaps it need not have, for the sun always shone there from a cloudless sky and the winds blew gently and it was always warm. You could slowly climb Kinnoull or saunter peacefully across the North Inch – or you could pull your rowboat softly up the Tay, in your shirt-sleeves, just any day at all. Or so it was in my father's and mother's day. Since I was not confident that this was still so, I did not visit Perth while it was cold and blowy in Edinburgh. But by mid-May the weather was so warm that I fell asleep on the bus somewhere past Stirling and failed to awaken till the Lindsays' street was a mile or two behind me. But it was a pleasant experience – to discover that I was suddenly and magically in Perth, and that it did not matter that I had missed the street. This, after all, was my home and I could find the Lindsays' street as easily as I could find Fourteenth Avenue or Douglas Road.

The Lindsays understood that there were certain things I had to do alone. On the several visits I made there, they would make preliminary arrangements and I could wander off whenever I wished. A visitor usually starts with cemeteries. They are histories for the living. As she searched for the location of the Murdoch stone, the clerk at Wellshill recalled my mother singing in Perth during the first war. It was a simple granite slab, as clean and fresh as when my grandmother was laid there, a few months before my mother sailed for Canada. If she had lived just three or four years more, she could have been cured of the pernicious anaemia that killed her. She would be eighty-six years of age now – and perhaps I would have met her. Helen, the wife of Harry Murdoch.

The Murdoch stone was simple, the same as its neighbours, but far down by the road I could see the slender marble column where my great-grandfather John and most of his fourteen children were buried. I sat on the low cement curb beneath the morning sun and read it in peace. Uncle John was here last September, swathed in his great

Mackintosh and his black Homburg, puffing on his pipe and muttering endless incantations. 'Grandfather was the first,' he said, 'in 1880. And Uncle David was the last, in 1937. I mind Aunt Nell. She was an awfie drinker but she was a kind soul. I mind o' the time she said we could keep all the eggs we could find in the barn, but when we got them home we discovered they were a' rotten.'

If I had roots, they were there in Wellshill – and out the Dunkeld Road at the Muirton. David Lindsay drove me there early one Sabbath morning. He dropped me where the railroad overpass crossed the road. He leaned over to me as I left and said, 'Tell your father you were at the Bogle Brig – but it's no' there now.' The Bogle Brig? Why yes, I recall the Bogle Brig, and that 'bogle' means 'ghost.' It was torn down and rebuilt. My father used to tell his children of the ghosties at the bridge that carried the railroad north to Aberdeen. To children, its alleged phantoms and its gloom made it a frightening spot. The new overpass is not frightening, at least not on a cloudy Sabbath morning. You can walk under it and up the dyke along the River Almond, which forms the northern boundary of the Muirton where my family farmed for a hundred years. The farm is not as large as I imagined it in my childhood. Far across the fields you can see the cluster of poplars and the stone house which Uncle David rebuilt because, as the story goes, he thought it vibrated. Perhaps it was the ghosties at the Bogle Brig. And then the barns and byres and off in the distance, over near the North Inch, the little cottage on the South Muirton farm where my father's Uncle John lived with his two sisters. My father said that the land there was good for growing beans and neeps. That biscuit barrel in our house – did it not have this John Morton's name on it? Did it not say, engraved into its silver, that this was a prize for his turnip crop?

Up here on the North Muirton, beneath my very feet, John and later David grew barley and oats and tatties and timothy hay – or so my father told me. And here surely is the site of the great rat slaughter on that blood-drenched autumn day so long ago. Two hundred.

Uncle John said, 'and nary a rat was found on the Muirton for many a year.' Walk along the Almond beneath leaden skies and south along the Tay, and here is Woody Island – and across the river, the Palace of Scone, from which the English stole the Stone of Destiny seven hundred years ago. I am behind the farmhouse – and farther south, behind the cottage – and here is the North Inch, on which Charles Edward Stewart trained his wild Highlanders. In that week two hundred years ago I could not have walked this expanse without being threatened by claymore or broadsword. Where would I be now if Charles had continued on to London? Where would I be now if James, the sixth son, had not died in 1891?

But I must hurry on. There is another nest of memories in the North Church. Sit where Maymie Lindsay says my father sat and look upward at the balcony where, Auntie Rachel told me a thousand times, she dandled the twins, my mother and my uncle, 'one on one knee, one on the other.' And at the choir where stern old Harry Murdoch stood and sang 'Comfort Ye' and 'Every Valley' and where my mother and my aunt, older now, sat casting sidelong glances at the young gentlemen of the town. I do not hear the sermon and when it is over, an elderly lady asks me if I am a visitor, and for just a moment emotion swells up within me and I cannot answer. A visitor? Why, if you go to Wellshill and the Muirton and… but it does not matter. I answer that my mother and father went to this church fifty years ago, and the nice old lady is not nearly as impressed as she should be. But there are others down at St Leonard's Church where Maymie has gathered my mother's and father's friends, and again names long forgotten come tumbling back into recollection.

I climb Kinnoull in the afternoon and see the Muirton and its barns and byres and the North Inch and the town and the Tay winding down through checkered fields to Dundee.

A visitor? To Perth? I have known it all my life. I have never left, though my father did.

| 1955 | **Ashley Courtenay** |

Let's Halt Awhile

PERTH – ROYAL GEORGE HOTEL. With an historic background the Royal George is a popular headquarters for business, pleasure and social occasions. Throughout the hotel there is every evidence of comfort, as, for example, in the Sundown cocktail lounge below stairs, and the ballroom on the first floor. An unusual feature for a British hotel is that en route to the dining-room glass panels give one a peep of the model kitchens. Note too, the interior decorations carried out by Peddie, a local artist.

With a car or without (good bus services radiate from Perth) one could spend an interesting week or more here, exploring some of Scotland's beauty spots.

F.Lic. W.T. from 9 gns. B.B. from 18/-. L 6/6. A.T. 2/6. D. 9/-. Rms: 52 (c.h. or e.f.). T.V. G. 30 cars, 1/6.

London 447. Dundee 21. Crieff 17. Tel. 890.

| 1960 | **Tom Weir** |

Scotland's Splendour

FOR THE CITY that was once the capital of Scotland, Perth has a wonderful air of belonging to the country rather than the town. That is its charm, especially on market days when the tackety boots and Scots tweeds proclaim that the farmers are in with a crop of lambs or a herd of good cattle beasts. The accent here is on quality, and if you know the value the world buyers put on Scottish cattle you would visit the annual bull sales and hear the fantastic prices bid for prizewinners that are raising the standard of cattle breeding all over the world.

Even the word 'Inch' has an association with the land, for it comes from the Gaelic innis, a long level grassland by the side of a stream. It was on the North Inch that the Battle of the Clans was fought, when sides were picked as in a football match and thirty men fought another thirty to the death. That was in the time of Robert III. Go to St John's Kirk and history does not seem so remote when you see the place where John Knox preached such a fiery sermon in 1559 that some six thousand reformers ransacked the town for images to destroy. The church is the same, except that the tower is now topped by a spire.

Unfortunately the work begun by Cromwell when he destroyed the Mercat Cross in 1651 was carried out too thoroughly by town-planning reformers when they rebuilt the city in the nineteenth century. They built the new Perth by sweeping away the old buildings regardless of their priceless link with history. Modern Perth, with its fine shops and spacious layout, is a tribute to them, but the zealous searcher will have to be content with plaques marking the places and faces in Scotland's story.

1962   **Douglas Eadie**

Two Poems About Perth
(from *Gambit* – Edinburgh University Review)

I – Low Tide at the Harbour

Oil elongates
Downstream, slates
The water duller
Now, too dull for spelling alphabets
Of colour:
So much for magic carpets.

A boat from Goole unloads
(On overtime).
Lizzie and Annie' corrodes,
Ex-president in foetal slime.

A gull bellyflaps
Into what's left for scraps.

II – Outside Saint John's Kirk

The bell bangs three o'clock
Official gold-chained beadle
Inaugurating time.

Others, unsuccessful, chime
Polite applause, wheedle
The hour's attention with smalltalk.

1963 **Lysbeth Brazier**

The Hill o' Kinnoull

I could sing ye a song o' Perth city sae grand,
O' this city that long was the first in the land,
O' the kings and the queens wha' hae walked hand in hand
In the fair city here by Kinnoull.
There are tales tae the gallant and tales tae the brave,
Songs tae the coward and odes tae the knave,
Each path that I tread has their mem'ries engraved
But I'll sing ye a song o' Kinnoull.

Chorus
The bonnie hill o' Kinnoull
Where the birds sing sae sweet in the mornin'.
Tae the people o' Perth there's nae mountain on earth
Can compare wi' the hill o' Kinnoull.

I could slip awa' quiet as the nicht settles doon,
The grey wraiths o' rime wrap the kirk steeple roon;
Tae wander sae high o'er the slumberin' toon
An' keep tryst wi' my love on Kinnoull.
The gloamin' sae saft does the valley enfold,
The lights o' the road mak a necklet o' gold,
And the auld River Tay maks a girdle sae bold
Aroon' the auld hill o' Kinnoull.

Mony a troth has been plighted up there,
And some midst the beauty found heartache sae sair;
But tae mony o' us it's a memory fair
Tae hae lingered and loved on Kinnoull.
True love may wander where primroses bloom,
And dream midst the perfume o' heather and broom,
Or kiss 'neath the light o' the auld harvest moon
That silvers the crest o' Kinnoull.

1963   **Lord Provost Dr Robert Ritchie**

The Lord Provost's Christmas Message in the
Perthshire Advertiser's Annual Review

TODAY WE SEE a newly heralded resurgence in the
economic life of Scotland. If all the many plans come to fruition the
face of Scotland is going to change greatly in the next generation.

Not only do we hope to see new industries and new ways of life transforming the social life of our country, but we can forecast considerable change in the face of many of our existing towns, including Perth. With great new development schemes such as that for the High Street/Thimblerow/Barracks area on the drawing boards, the rebuilding of Perth will march along with the rebuilding of Scotland.

We can only hope that this great new surge of enterprise will not be confined to central Scotland to the exclusion of other areas such as Perth, and the Town Council will continue to be active in placing before industrialists the advantages of this City. We will also do all we can to encourage existing Perth industries to expand.

We have seen this year yet again a great expansion in the tourist industry and in the number of visitors who are coming to Perth and Perthshire. This new influx, coupled with the natural increase in motor travel, is creating even greater problems in traffic control and the Town Council are now considering in detail proposals for relieving congestion in Perth streets. It is an alarming thought to realise that within ten years the traffic in Perth streets will be doubled. To strike a fair balance between the claims of motorists, pedestrians and the owners of business premises in the town, is no easy task, but one which the Town Council has to face.

1965   **Moray McLaren**

The Shell Guide to Scotland

PERTH is alternatively known as the Fair City. The visitor to the place would do well to agree with the alternative as an axiom, if he would not fall foul of the vehement, but courteous, unanimity of the citizens. Yet, if you had the temerity to be objective, you might say that it is not clear whether it is the city itself that is fair, or its setting, or both. Natives of sensibility (and they are by no means few) might admit that there is not much of architectural distinction left to command the awed attention of the incomer. The ancient kirk of St John Baptist, one of the noblest of the great Scottish burghal churches of the 15th century, with its spire 'as clean as a hound's tooth', is by far the rarest of the relics, both in antiquity and in beauty. But it is condemned (as it seems, for perpetuity) to look out on the broad and ill-mannered rear of a 19th century City Hall, and, on either side, it is hemmed in by warehouses, public houses, and factories, with nothing to commend them to the eye. Elsewhere, tucked away between modern frontages, sweetly-curved small windows throw light on antiques (in South Street) and, until a recent most recent demolition in the High Street, on ironmongery. If you hunt for them, you will come upon vestiges of the town houses that belonged to a now long-dead nobility; well-proportioned gables recall a past more tenderly resolved to combine elegance with function. Solidity is fused with grace in the terraces and places that confront the green magnificence of the riverside inches. These terraces, in particular Rose Terrace, are reminiscent of the Edinburgh New town style, and are an example of how that noble style continued to flourish and push its way up the east of Scotland deep into the 19th century. A cheer is due no less for the new (1960) ferro-concrete Queen's Bridge than for Smeaton's old (1771) masterpiece in rose-red sandstone, farther up-river. The attractions of the mid-20th century City Centre (between South Street and High Street) may be considered dubious.

But take a look at Perth as you come up from the south, over 'Necessity Brae' (which joins the main road from Glasgow at Cherry-bank), or in from the east, or best of all from the summit of Kinnoull Hill (729 ft), and the prospect is surely stirring: that of the varied, natural grandeur enfolding the place, but not less, perhaps, that of the place itself, spired and rocky, solid and studiously compact, emanating an immemorial fidelity to its bridges which (if it did not impoverish the merchants in its medieval guilds) well served the security and wealth of bygone Scotland through many centuries.

Or walk up the river from the old bridge, look around and marvel at the continuing pleasance of the modern scene. Colonial cricketers, with (as the locals are sure) as much aesthetic discrimination as athletic distinction, have been known to testify that they never play in more splendid surroundings than those of Scotland's premier County Club on the North Inch.

Otherwise Perth is exceptionally well-furnished for its size. It has a much more than passable art gallery and museum (George Street). It has the well-stocked Sandeman Library (Kinnoull Street). It has the oldest-established repertory theatre in Scotland, from which many have emerged to stardom in the West End and on television. Of late it has achieved its own orchestra and choral society, which can endure the most stringent critic. It has learned societies of many sorts. It has a mint of money at its disposal for cultural and charitable objects. It is abundantly rich in open spaces and recreational facilities of every sort.

Poverty nowhere obtrudes: the Town Council has a housing record of enterprise, if not of aesthetic excellence, that can bear comparison with any other. It is a comfortable place, and its people look comfortable, as indeed all but a minority are. Generally they look no less tidy than comfortable. And, by and large, they are contented and law-abiding. They have solid, if unexciting, reasons for their content.

1965 **Peter Martin**

A Dog Called Perth

WE WERE JUST BACK from an entire summer in Scotland, our minds brimming with its romantic landscape's magic of hills, mountains, lochs, mountain breezes and wild echoes. We had also visited the lovely town of Perth in the Lowlands, on the Great North Road between Edinburgh and Inverness, near the mouth of Scotland's longest river, the Tay. Mild and civilised in its outlook, it has been called the most congenial place to live in Britain. In Scotland, in fact, we found much of the spirit of romance and adventure with which we hoped to keynote our marriage.

1969 Douglas Eadie

Perspective on Perth (from *The Scottish Field*)

The River

PERTH BEGINS with the river. The Tay flows out of the Highlands 37 miles to the north, and alternately winds and rushes over Strathmore, gathering the Isla and the Almond on the way. Just where it starts being tidal, as it passes between the western buttress of the Sidlaws and the gentler rises of Gask, is Perth. Then it rounds Moncreiffe Island and leaves the town, broadening into its estuary and the North Sea away beyond Dundee.

Statistically, the Tay is impressive – more than 90 miles long and carrying to the sea the largest volume of water of any British river. And to look at, in its last 30 miles or so anyway, it's even more impressive, so much so that in most lights you would want to call it silvery, and McGonagall did. The Romans, according to others before Sir Walter Scott put it into rhyme, were reminded of the Tiber, and a local landowner around the turn of the 19th century into the 20th thought it so much like the Rhine that he had two ruins built, one on Kinnoull Hill, the other on Binn Hill, in the style of robber barons' Rhenish hideouts. *Ecce Tiber, voila das Rhein*, Perth's ole man river.

People fish in it for fish, salmon particularly, men and wee boys, commercially and for pleasure, and one man, James Abernethy fishes it for pearls. People sail boats on it, mostly for pleasure now, though some 300 small cargo boats ply in and out of the harbour every year. People walk along it, watch birds on it, knock golf balls into it. Not many people swim in it.

The Bridges

PERTH GREW where it did on the west bank of the river because trade and military routes through lush valleys and hill gaps from west to east and south to north conjoined there, and because there also was the lowest bridgeable point on the river. Barely so. A fast-flowing river, the Tay until quite recently was troublesomely liable to flood. Now afforestation and hydro-electric operations keep it in more even check, but in 1210 the castle and most of the town were destroyed by a flood, and early efforts to establish a strong and permanent bridge came to grief in 1573, 1582 and 1589.

In 1600 James VI at Holyrood ordered yet another bridge over the Tay at Perth. It was to be 'a most precious jewel of our kingdom, and a work profitable and primely necessary to our whole kingdom and dominion, and for the suppression of rebels and such as are viciously affected, most commodious, and also keeping the one half of the kingdom, with the other half thereof in faith, obedience, duty and office, towards us their kings, in our kingdom and dominion.' This bridge was completed in 1617, and removed by the Tay in 1620.

Thomas Smeaton's 1771 bridge, however, paid for by a subscription taken among Perth merchants and manufacturers, is still standing, and into its west end are cut the high water marks of subsequent floods. A 10-year-old sister road bridge spans the river 200 yards downstream and a late 19th century iron railway bridge carries the Glasgow-Aberdeen expresses across the river at the south end of the historical town centre.

Plaques and History

IN THE LAST 200 years Perth has lived on the fringes of history, just keeping in touch: a prison (still used as such) built to house French p.o.w.s during the Napoleonic Wars, Garibaldi paying a social visit; and now the odd political conference passing resolutions which make the papers but probably not the history books...

Yet right up to the death of Scottish history in 1746 (murdered by whom?), Perth was in there at the centre. Whenever the name cropped up in school history books you felt a kick of something between excitement at the grand affair that had happened in Perth and disappointment that nothing happened now.

There were Romans, and English pinching the Stone from nearby Scone, and Wallace sneaking into Perth on an amorous escapade and escaping out again and hiding in a cave among the Kinnoull cliffs: 650 years later, schoolboys go looking for this cave, don't find it, and feel that history may sometimes be a cheat.

Bruce took Perth. Kings lived in Perth, in the days before it was safe enough to live in Edinburgh, so that Perth was once Capital, and that is why the Perth Lord Provost walks second only to Edinburgh on occasions of national dignity. There was one king, the poet James I, who died violently at Perth.

There was John Knox, preaching the sermon that caused a riot that caused the Reformation that caused idolatry, hagiolatry and all sorts of other things to be put an end to that caused the name of the town to be changed from St. Johnstoun back to Perth, the Gaelic-Pictish name (Aber-tay) the Romans knew as Bertha. St. John's, the Kirk where it all started, is still standing, hallowed, much-renovated, and remarkably peaceful.

Before Knox, there was the Battle of the Clans, a desperate do Sir Walter Scott reduced to an encounter of indecent gallantry and decent cowardice. There are plaques up on the walls of two houses said

to have been lived in respectively by the Fair Maid of Perth and by Hal
o' the Wynd, her beau.

There are so many plaques, brass, bronze, gold paint, marble
– it's as though generations of Perth burgesses could have had had
history but preferred to seal themselves into their own present with a
multitude of plaques. Besides St. John's, the 15th century Pitheavlis
Castle and a few old houses, it's all plaques: Montrose, Cromwell,
Bonnie Prince Charlie, castles, battles, murders, disasters, events of a
merely romantic nature, famous writers like Ruskin, John Buchan and
Gavin Douglas, names commemorated but no longer famous.

The Present

IN THE PRESENT, Perth is a relatively small town, population around the 42,000 mark. But just as some black birds are too
big to be blackbirds, so Perth is too big a small town to be smalltown.
It has its own traditions and independences. The fact that it's geograph-
ically nodal means that express trains leave London, destination Perth,
and that puts the two places on some kind of par. Young men and
women leave Perth, but other young men and women come into Perth.
Hardly enough of them though, at least in the last ten years, and Sir
Frank Mears and Partners, the Edinburgh planning consultants, were
recently called in to advise on the situation.

Two sentences from their preliminary report accurately char-
acterise Perth's economy: the present – 'A prosperous and far spread
agricultural community looks to Perth for many of its needs, and so
provides a stable foundation for the town's main function of distribu-
tive, retail, miscellaneous and professional services'; the future –
'So long as Perth performs the function of a regional capital there can
be no question of its providing at the same time a large industrial
labour force, and the industrial sector would be regarded as a regulator
increasingly needed to absorb the anticipated changeover of employ-

ment structure as a result of the possible rundown of railways and the reduction of employment in the service industries.'

Perth earns a lot of dollars with Dewar's, Bell's and several smaller companies blending and bottling in the town. Pullar's, the cleaners and dyers, used to be important enough to have telephone number Perth 1. Moncreiff Glassworks produces high-grade laboratory glassware from Loch Aline sand.

Biggest single employer in Perth is the General Accident Fire and Life Assurance Corporation, which has had its headquarters there since 1885. It's the hundreds of 'G. A.' white-collar workers who give Perth its pre-dominant mid-lower-middle class outlook and sense of comfort. These and the shopkeepers, many of whom have businesses as old-established as the G. A. Rattray's the tobacconists, for instance, who supply J. B. Priestly, and, it's rumoured, Harold Wilson.

A more dynamic outlook to the future has just emerged than was prevalent ten years ago. As a result a recently formed Tayside jute manufacturing consortium has come into Perth to keep alive a traditional but languished fabric industry, and G. R. Electronics, a firm producing electronic circuits, has been enticed to the city.

As a market town, Perth has more hotel accommodation than Dundee, two and a half times its size. Every February, Spanish gutturals mingle with Texas drawls for the bull sales, and the tiny sale ring, crowded on all sides, seems a bit like the Alamo. In the future, Perth hopes to trade in people as much as in livestock, and a full-time tourist officer was recently employed to sell the town as the ideal touring centre it is. Pubs and restaurants are booming, and Reo Stakis has bought the Old City Mills to make what he can of them.

Recreation and Sport

WRITING IN 1796, a Rev. James Scott reported that 'Some of the public amusements common in other places are to be found in Perth. Among these, particular notice may be taken of the amusements of the theatre. Players occasionally come to Perth, and sometimes they remain very long.' True then, that's still true now: Perth repertory theatre has been going since 1935 and is a public thing that gains and wanes in people's confidence as 'difficult' or 'controversial' plays spice to a greater or less extent the staple of well-tried favourites, pantomimes and summer shows.

There's also a lot of music and song around Perth, with an amateur orchestra, chamber music, and competitive festival, but some prefer for their leisure something less harmonious than Mozart and more dramatic than Noel Coward. For such people, the significant double H of the past year has not been Hubert Humphrey, nor, indeed, Harry Hood, but Henry Hall, whose thirty goals last season brought himself into the running for an international cap and St. Johnstone F. C. to a likely place in next season's Fair Cities Cup European tournament. Strange to go back to Muirton Park after a lapse of several seasons and hear a 500-strong youngsters' chorus singing 'On the road to You-rupp we shall not be moved.' Stranger still to find yourself joining in the 'Hall-ay-loo-ya' chorus after another well-taken goal.

At the end of each football season the punters of many Scottish towns just have to breathe hard and aestivate till the beginning of the next, but Perth slips smoothly into the calmer spectacle of cricket. The North Inch is where the Perthshire County XI play. G. K. Chesterton said that the English, not being a mystical people, invented cricket to give themselves some idea of eternity, but the river that a very big six hit eastwards might land in provides Perth people with a sufficient notion of that, so North Inch cricket matches tend to be short and snappy. That's how the Big Daddies of Scottish cricket like it: get the visitors out and top their score between closing time and opening time.

Elsewhere and at other times on the Inches, South as well as North, the rattle of infant balls against bats unwieldily out of proportion to the size of the batsmen ensures the continuity of the species. There's also rugby, coarse rather than game, with Perthshire Academicals celebrating this year their centenary, hunt-racing at nearby Scone, the recently opened Bell's indoor sports stadium, golf and bowls, a championship standard swimming pool and an ice rink where this year's world curling championships were held. Afterwards, a Canadian reported in his Winnipeg newspaper that he'd found hoar-frost on his hotel toilet seat, and if any publicity's good publicity that's one up for Perth tourism.

For that very important class of sporting people, young lovers, there's Kinnoull Hill, with trees and heather and broad views as dreamily expansive as the future they hope for, and cliffs as precarious as love itself. And if that's lyrical to the point of stupidity, put it down to nostalgia, and put down to discretion silence about the private nooks there also are on the hill.

The Fair City

IT'S A MOOT POINT whether people create environment or environment people, but one way and another Perth seems about right for its citizens and vice versa. It's called the Fair City, and that slightly pallid compliment is also very appropriate. Architecturally, there are some nice things – St. John's Kirk, the old waterworks, a couple of terraces of merchant-professional class houses that look much more dignified than complacent; the museum and galleries and the neo-gothic encrusted imitation of St. Giles in Edinburgh testify to a 19th century sense that you had to keep up with imperial grandeur. But generally speaking, Perth people have knocked down and rebuilt with each generation, and top priority is given to utility rather than good looks. So that the recently formed Perth Civic Trust provides an overdue lobby in the town for the preservationist case.

It's probably impossible, going back to Perth, not to be a bit irritated. The sense of irritation has little to do with Perth. It's just that the exercise of memory gets more difficult with each successive visit. Buildings disappear as well as people, the bars change from dark wood and coal fires to Formica and plush. When your first environment alters, it's as if your own security were being threatened from the rear. But then, you walk out over the North or South Inch (the tree-dotted expanses of flat grassland stretching west from the river and limiting the old town to the north and south) and these are much the same as they were. And the river's the same. And over the bridges Kinnoull Hill's much the same, though the well-heeled modern houses are climbing slowly to the roadend.

1971 **Nigel Tranter**

The Heartland

IT IS NOT ACCURATE to call Perth a Highland town; but it is an ideal gateway to the Highlands. As far as situation, surroundings and many prospects are concerned, it is well deserving of its proud title of the Fair City.

Yet the town itself is not beautiful – not to be compared with Stirling, for instance, however much more convenient a municipality. The reasons are twofold. First is that undulation of site is necessary to provide beauty and prospect; and Perth is built on a flat. Second, great as was the city's architectural heritage from the past, practically all of it has been swept away and replaced by, in the main, the utilitarian and the humdrum. This is perhaps less than fair, for there are many fine modern or semi-modern buildings; but compared with what has been lost and destroyed, these scarcely count.

Because of its safe and rich position, and its proximity to Scone, the first capital of the united Scotland of Kenneth MacAlpine – the Abbey of which became Scotland's Westminster – Perth came to contain the most important concentration of religious establishments in the kingdom. It is not quite true to say, as is often done, that it was once itself the capital of Scotland, because James I chose to make it his favourite place of residence. By such standards Turnberry, Dunfermline, Cardross, Linlithgow and Falkland all might be called one-time capitals. Stirling was the true capital, the principal palace and fortress and permanent seat of government, until Edinburgh superseded it. But it is very strange that Perth did not become the ecclesiastical metropolis; that St Andrews should have gained this eminence instead. For St Andrews was isolated, inconvenient and at first had nothing like so many monasteries, priories, nunneries and so on, nor of course the proximity to Scone. It had its traditional connection with St Andrew and his relics, of course, the patron saint; but this seems insufficient, especially when Perth was in the centre of greatest influence of the old Celtic Church. Perhaps this was part of the trouble, as far as the Romish polity was concerned. Here is no place to go into this problem; but it is strange indeed that Perth in fact was not even the seat of a bishop. Yet here, under the eye of Scone the great religious houses proliferated, the monastic institutions of the Black Friars, the Grey Friars, the White Friars, the Carthusians and so on, in splendid, sometimes princely establishments, with nunneries, hospices, chapels and churches to match. Alas, all are gone – although there is still a modern Roman Catholic monastery across the river on the side of Kinnoull Hill. Happily, the great St John's Kirk of Perth, and the episcopal cathedral of St Ninian, carry on after a fashion the ecclesiastical tradition – though the latter is the seat of the See of Dunkeld, not of Perth.

The title of Fair City, therefore, is slightly suspect, in the second word's implication, as of the first – since a city is usually indicative of a very large community or the seat of its own cathedral. The population here is only 41,000. Yet, by any standards, this is a major Scots town, quite apart from being the capital of one of the really great counties, a place of resounding fame, notable character and very real interest, even charm. Its attractions are innumerable. Although it was a walled town in the Middle Ages – indeed, besieged and captured, in person, by Robert the Bruce – only a 50-foot section of the old walling remains, down a narrow lane at George Street. There are some foundations of the Speygate Tower opposite the Greyfriars Burial-ground in Canal Street.

Any description of Perth should almost certainly begin at St John's Kirk, since this is not only the oldest extant building but the reason for the place's medieval name of St John's-toun. It stands in the centre of the town, all the streets seeming to enshrine it. Dedicated to John the Baptist, there was a church on this site as early as 1126, when its revenues were granted to the new Abbey of Dunfermline.

This great church is really the heart and centre of Perth. There was a castle once, to the north, but it was never as important as that church. Around St John's the streets are laid out in notably regular and systematic fashion unusual in an ancient town in Scotland. The main two, running east and west, are South Street and High, or North, Street. St John's Square lies between the two; and here, west of the church and the City Hall, is an attractive new development, a traffic-free shopping precinct centred round a replica of the old Mercat Cross – the latter erected in 1913 in memory of King Edward VII.

1975 **Duncan Fraser**

Discovering East Scotland

PERTH IS THE kind of town which appeals in different ways to different people. To some it conjures up a vision of thousands upon thousands of bottles waiting to be filled, to boost Britain's export drive. Others think of snell February winds and a sale ring, with princely bulls lumbering endlessly round, the aristocrats of the Aberdeen-Angus and Shorthorn breeds. Many of these bulls, like the bottles, will be going to the far ends of the earth and still their buyers will come back to Perth for more.

Owners of coasting vessels tend to think of the town as a seaport, though it is inland twenty miles and more, on the banks of the Tay. Architects know it better for its Georgian architecture – like Edinburgh's New Town in miniature, beautiful and impersonal. Garden lovers think of Branklyn in June – that two acre garden which the late Mrs Renton created, alongside the busy Dundee road and yet seemingly miles from anywhere. Some say it is the finest garden of its size in Europe and certainly in Scotland it has no equal. But to most people Perth means something quite different from any of these. Though it is one of the flattest of towns, it gives them a picture of mountains, for this is their gateway to the Highlands.

1976   **Billy Connolly**

Billy Connolly: The Authorized Version

I LOVE JUST travelling through some of the places, the names still mean so much to me... Perth, where they have this Royal British Hotel, and they would have just the initials of it on the wall: R. B. And I used to picture it as a Rhythm and Blues Hotel... like you'd go inside and there would be all these black guys playing their guitars in the lounge and jamming away together. Can you imagine that, in the middle of Perth?

*   *   *

1976   **Ian Finlay**

The Central Highlands

Perth and the North

THIS CHAPTER-HEADING may not accurately describe the scope of what follows, but I selected it for its nostalgic ring. Perth is the ancient gateway to the Central Highlands, and when I was a small boy the name had romantic overtones, especially in the mouths of station porters in Edinburgh banging doors as departure time approached. 'Perth and the North!' they chanted above the hiss of steam. The gigantic flickering of the cantilevers of the Forth Bridge brought the next anticipatory thrill, and Glenfarg seemed to be the very doorstep to the hills. But the climax came with grinding brakes as the olive green locomotive and its red-brown coaches snaked slowly into the long main-line platform of Perth station, and everywhere was a stir for the change into the strange green Highland Railway coaches, into which they were loading lunch-baskets. Perth in those days was almost a frontier town. The North British and the Caledonian Railways' jurisdiction ended there, and one passed into the keeping of a company whose rolling stock, whose very castellated bridges, had almost a foreign look. For a child it was much more exciting and, I suspect, for adults too. It is all much too easy to-day. The motorway now brings Perth within an hour of Edinburgh, and we can be among the pine-clad foothills around Birnam almost before the day's journey has begun. R. L. Stevenson's wise words, that it is better to travel hopefully than to arrive, are forgotten in this age.

However, the first glimpse of Perth still is impressive enough. The road swerves round a bend, and there is the town spread out below. The setting is splendid – a far rim of blue hills ringing a pleasance of green fields and woods, with the bends of the River Tay flashing in the sun.

In spite of its bustling streets, it is a cross-roads from south to north and from west to east, as yet without a by-pass. There is a lingering air of early-nineteenth century values in the quieter corners which is refreshing to experience. Partly, of course, it stems from the fact that so many of its buildings belong to this time, give or take a decade or two, from the Bridge built by Smeaton in 1772 and the barracks of about the same period to the Perth Academy of 1805 and the infirmary of 1836. But it also comes from the tweeds and sprinkling of deerstalkers, the scent of cigar smoke more specially at the time of the world-famous bull-sales, second-hand bookshops where one may still occasionally find a bargain, antique-shops which are rather less ravished by the wholesale export trade than those further south. It is still possible to imagine John Ruskin playing in the riverside garden over at Bridgend. And speaking of books and authors, there is still a flourishing Literary and Antiquary Society, which I once had the honour of addressing.

1976   **Jack House**

Pride of Perth

PERTH IS A PROUD CITY and still remembers that it was the capital of Scotland until King James III transferred the seat of monarchy to Edinburgh in 1482. And Perth can trace its history back to the days of the Romans, for General Agricola established a camp there. At the beginning of the thirteenth century Perth was a flourishing city when Glasgow was a mere village in the shadow of its cathedral.

During the eighteenth century the principal manufacture in Perth was linen and the Perth merchants dealt directly with no fewer than forty-six watermills within four miles of Perth, all engaged in bleaching and printing linen and cotton. Then came the slump and even the Duke of Wellington's victory at Waterloo couldn't bring the citizens of Perth out of the doldrums.

By 1825 things had improved only a little. The population of Perth was just under 20,000 and one report said, 'The poor in Perth are numerous'.

1979 **David Graham-Campbell**

Portrait of Perth, Angus and Fife

Perth – 'The Fair City'

PERTH – formerly St Johnstown – is a fair city to live in. It is true that it might have been even fairer, had more been done to preserve the treasures of the past. Many fine buildings have been allowed to fall into decay and then have had to be pulled down, because they had become dangerous, or to make way for something more habitable, or more useful, or just more in keeping with passing fashions. What would one not give to have the sixteenth-century Gowrie House back again, or the Blackfriars' Monastery or the Charterhouse? One splendid medieval building remains, the High Kirk of St John's, 'one of the noblest burghal churches that have survived to us in Scotland'; and there is much of interest from the eighteenth and early nineteenth centuries: the King James Hospital, the Waterworks (now imaginatively converted into a well-equipped Information Centre), Marshall Place overlooking the South Inch, and, beside the North Inch, Rose Terrace with the well-proportioned Old Academy building as its centre piece.

Yet it is not for its old buildings, as a rule, that a man chooses his home town, for few people can actually live in old houses; it is rather for the situation and the friendliness of its people. The casual tourist passing hurriedly through may find the High Street crowded on a Saturday afternoon, especially in the height of the summer, or the motorist be confused by its complex system of one-way streets, but he should wait till Sunday morning, and stand at the west end of South Street and look down its wide spaciousness to the trees of Kinnoull Hill; or, from the other end, on the Queen's Bridge, look back along South Street, again to green fields; or up the broad Tay to Smeaton's Bridge (1766–1771) and the North Inch beyond; or downstream to Moncrieffe Island and the King James VI golf course. One of the great attractions of Perth, as of the larger Aberdeen, is its compactness, so that the countryside is always close at hand, and, because Perth like Aberdeen is embraced by hills, the green is visible from nearly everywhere. Perth's crowning glory is, of course, its river and the two open spaces that complement it, the South Inch astride the road to Edinburgh, and the North Inch with its magnificent beeches and elms and chestnuts.

If Perth has a past to live down, it has a strong social sense today. Its Civic Trust and the Friends of St John's and its own Local Authority have done much to see that its citizens should be aware of, and preserve, their heritage. But vigilance is still necessary: and an elected councillor was recently reported as saying that the Civic Trust 'is as outmoded as the House of Lords'.

The same civic sense is evident in private life too, in, say, the little gardens of Florence Place or the aptly named Rose Crescent, and in the enthusiasm which gives Perth not only a fortnight's Festival of the Arts but, throughout the year, thriving amateur orchestral and choral societies, and a professional repertory theatre company with a deservedly high reputation. The local ice rink is the home of international curling; and the swimming baths and Bell's Sports Centre, the river and the Inches provide facilities for every sort of recreation.

Golf has always figured largely in the life of Perth. According to the kirk records of 1604, one Robertson had to sit in the seat of repentance for 'playing at the gowf on the Sabbath on the North Inch at the time of preaching afternoon', and the game has been played there ever since. The Royal Perth Golfing Society, now combined with the City and County Club, was founded in 1824 and has comfortable premises in Atholl Crescent. The King James VI club also played on the North Inch at first.

Horse racing goes back as far as golf on the North Inch, but today it takes place at Scone, the autumn meeting being followed by the hunt ball. Also on the North Inch are the headquarters of the Perthshire Cricket Club, and the Perth Rugby Football Club, while not far away is Muirton Park, the St Johnstone football ground.

One last, and rather picturesque, feature of Perth is its company of uniformed High Constables, an institution shared only by Holyrood, Edinburgh and the Port of Leith. They were in existence before 1466 as a sort of police force to enable the city magistrates to enforce law and order, but they have not been called out in that capacity since 1843 when some soldiers ran amok. Now, like the Queen's Bodyguard for Scotland, theirs is a dignified rather than a martial role.

1984   Dr William H. Findlay

Heritage of Perth

A FAMOUS FILM DIRECTOR has said, 'Every country has its own mist'. Couldn't the claim be made that in Scotland every town has its own mist – its own atmosphere? The River Tay as it passes through Perth settles this tribute upon us on its way to the sea, a rare heritage that changes from day to day and season to season but never palls. But is the appreciation of this available only to those who are accessible to aesthetic impressions? I think not. More people than we realise have this sensitivity.

The Reverend David D. Ogston

Rehearsal

Cameron was gweed eneuch
Tae gie's a lift faan
We wis ready for Wellshill.
'We'll bring ye back,' he said.

So aff we set in the hearse,
The fower o's: the driver
An Cameron in the front.
An the twa o's in the back.

There wisna jist a lot o room
In the wee seat. My knees
Wis a bit scuffy for clearance
An I hid naebody tae spik till.

My heid wis echteen inch
Awa fae polished timmer,
Bress and tassel. I suppose
Ye could say I wis boxed in.

Up at the grave-side I wad
Warsie oot, bit funny – been
An shooder stuck an baith
Ma feet wis sleepin.

'Dae ye want a haun oot?'
Says Cameron, so I grippit
His haun an loot him rive me

On to solid grun.

Actors, they say, afore the play
Gets yokit, plot positions
On the boords wie chalk
So's they will ken their places.

Some ither day, faan I get helpit
Fae a hearse, they'll be bumbased
At sic a smooth performance.
'He's deen't afore,' they'll say.

1985　**Roy Kerridge**

Twenty Years of Perth

BY COINCIDENCE I have visited the beautiful city of Perth, former capital of Scotland, once in every ten years. On my first visit, in 1965, I stayed at the Salutation Hotel in South Street, near the river. This is the oldest hotel in Perth, founded in 1699. There are brightly painted statues above the door, and a plaque that commemorates a distinguished guest, Bonnie Prince Charlie. Last week I returned to the Salutation, and found it to be exactly the same. I no longer yearned to be a member of the exclusive night club behind the stairs, but the club was still there. There was still a roaring fire in the entrance hall as in the old style of inns. After being caught in the rain, it was pleasant to pull a chair up to the fire and dry off, with jovial commercial travellers for company. The mantelpiece only needed a clock with bills behind it to be completely home-like.

From the dining room window there is a Georgian-perspective-drawing view of the symmetrical streets outside. A clean, gracious city, with few modern additions, Perth resembles Bath, Cheltenham and the better parts of Brighton. The council houses on the outskirts are tall, shining white and rapidly being bought by their tenants. I noticed no unsightly blocks of flats. A gentle, well-mannered city by day, Perth is brawling and dangerous at night when the pubs turn out. Church spires meet the eye at every turn, and on Sunday mornings crowds emerge from the kirks.

There is a long promenade by the River Tay, with its two great bridges, Perth and Queen's. At intervals, inscribed on stones, are memorials to Old Perth. One of these marked the spot where, in 1633, King Charles of England had visited Perth and been entertained in a house built on floating timbers, from whence he watched 13 morris dancers prancing along the embankment.

On my first visit, I stood entranced on Perth Bridge in the half-light of evening. I had never been so far north before, and I gazed in all directions. The civic buildings of Perth, their contours bathed in orange lamplight, seemed wonderfully strange. So did the homegoing crowds, striding briskly beneath the plane trees. I felt like the innocent hero of a Robert Louis Stevenson story.

Soon I was to find the vennels, the old-fashioned stone alleyways that honeycomb the city. At the end of one vennel, on a wall, a rough black and white picture of a bishop's castle had been painted, to give an impression of mediaeval Perth. By day, in 1965 as now, housewives discussed Christian doctrine in broad local accents, as well as quoting such authors as Stevenson and Congreve. At night, respectably-dressed men reeled about swearing. Once I saw a long queue of pleasant-looking men, women and children outside a great illuminated hall with classical columns. From their benign expressions and air of decency, I assumed that they were going to an evangelical rally. No, it was to a wrestling match! In England, a wrestling crowd would have looked far more brutal, but such things seemed measured by a different scale here where real, not simulated, brutality took place in after-hours vennel fights.

In 1975, on my second visit, I stayed not at the Salutation but at South Inch, where witches once were burned. Here a row of bed-and-breakfast houses looked over the flat, grassy Inch (or park) to the hills and mountains on the far side of the Tay. One house, with a brass doorknocker in the shape of a piper, had a flimsy cardboard sign fixed to a pole near the gate.

'Mrs McBain's Transport Accomodation House,' I read, so I climbed the steps and banged the door with the brass piper. Soon I was allocated to Bed Number Four in the Long Dorm. This was my own name for the room where lorry drivers slept, their beds packed in like sardines. The houses facing the Inch had been built for fine ladies and gentlemen, and the Long Dorm had a most aristocratic ceiling of white plasterwork in foliated designs. I made friends with a dark curly-haired lorry driver with craggy features. He came from Berwick on Tweed, and spoke with quiet pleasures of his favourite fishing spots among the trees on the banks of that river.

At breakfast in the kitchen next morning, I found the Clan McBain to be 'Scots Nat' in their views. Scottish oil was still a talking point.

'Where is the wealth from the oil?' my landlady demanded, fixing me with a sardonic eye.

'I haven't seen it! It's not in private hands,' I protested, as she looked me sceptically up and down.

'A wee bomb wud dae England the most guid, Ah'm thinkin,' she concluded. 'Not to hurt a'body, of course.'

Now, ten years later, such attitudes seem entirely to have vanished. Rebellious young people of Perth tend to be neo-Mods, with Union Jacks stitched to the back of their khaki jackets. I saw two Mod boys, in miniature '1964 gear', out walking by the Tay with their father.

'Angus came burstin intae class shoutin "Heroin deal!"', one chirpy Union Jack-clad 15-year-old told his friends in a juke box cafe. Excitedly they discussed heroin, which seemed to hold a fascination for them, as one of the few things that all teachers disapproved of. Hairy druggy teachers who smoke reefers and recommend drugs 'if not abused' are adamant in their hatred of heroin. There has been a widely circulated magazine called *Sniffin' Glue*, but no one writes well of heroin, or 'smack', the Last Forbidden Fruit. Authority-figures, such as Sixties pop stars, denounce it in public, heightening its romantic attraction to the young. Those who talk and dream of drugs have not necessarily ever seen any, and I have no idea whether or not there is any heroin in Perth.

Before going to Perth this year, I had spent a few days with Farmer Chawbacon at Starveacre Farm in Staffordshire, trudging through the snow. The further north I traversed, the finer the weather, and as I sauntered along the Tayside prom, the sun shone down, soft breezes soothed my brow and I was disturbed only by the discordant cries of anguished skiers from England who had hoped to find snow. In St Ninian's Cathedral, Atholl Street, shafts of sunlight across the dark roof beams made me feel I was in a sacred forest grove. Such pagan thoughts may not have pleased the Saint, who was the Christian son of a fourth-century Scottish chieftain.

'Sixty-five, 'seventy-five or 'eighty-five, there have been no great changes made in Perth. Twenty years ago, on my first visit, I was engaged in reading the Bible from cover to cover. This left no time for Sir Walter Scott, so I was puzzled to see notices everywhere pointing out the Fair Maid of Perth's house. Who was this Fair Maid? Intrigued, I followed the signs and soon came to a small, round, tower-like building constructed in the Nineties on the site of an old dwelling. It was the Fair Maid of Perth's house.

Downstairs, the Maid's successors were selling expensive tartan materials. Upstairs was an art gallery full of modern doodlings. They were presided over by a young longhaired Englishman. Another long-haired Englishman, with an air of oafish knowingness, was saying to the first one: 'eh, yeh, you can see what the artist's getting at, you know what I mean?'

147

Now I had just reached in my reading, the famous letter from St Paul to the Corinthians where the Apostle declares, with great and lasting effect, that women are to wear hats in church but men are not. He also added that long hair in a man was shameful. Still, I thought, perhaps the Caveliers had redemed long hair since Biblical times. So I approached the long-haired curator and asked him if he knew who the Fair Maid of Perth might be. He seemed stunned at this query for a moment, but quickly rallied.

'Some old girl,' he hazarded. 'Some old girl who used to live 'ere, I suppose. No, hang on. Wouldn't be called 'Fair' if she was some old dear, would she? No, some young girl, must o' been. A right darling she must o' been, with all the boys after 'er. Yeh'

'Thank you.' I said, feeling that perhaps St Paul had known what he was talking about after all.

Nearby, in Mill Street, I found that the long grey mill house with its immense water-wheel had been made into a pub. So I sat in dark, plush surroundings sipping my bitter lemon and watching the wheel splashing round and round like the Wheel of Time. Ten revolutions of the years and I would be back in Perth, another ten and I would again return. But I hope that the cycle may be speeded up, for I don't want to wait until the new Naughty Nineties before I can visit Perth once more.

1986   R. F. Mackenzie

A Search For Scotland

FOR CENTURIES the people of the Carse watched cargoes going down the river from Perth, salmon, sheep, gloves, paper, and, up river, flax, 'lintseed', porter, cheese, groceries, wood, iron, lime. Some of the ships were bound for Petrograd and the Hansa towns, and Hansa merchants visited Perth. Linen from London was bleached on Perth bleachfields. Like inquisitive cats, people were prying into the secrets of natural substances, and seeing what they could make of them. the first mill in Scotland for crushing lintseed into linseed oil was built at Huntingtower, two miles away. The oil was used for paint and printers' ink, varnish, tablecloths and floor-cloths, glue, knife-handles and in medicine for burns. Perth foundry built the first iron ship on the east coast. When the young ask us, 'What makes Scotland tick?' some of these stories would help them to appreciate what kind of characters their grandfathers and grandmothers were long ago. They're not likely to make much of the information that James I was killed in Perth and that James III made Perth the official capital and that it was in Perth that Bonnie Prince Charlie proclaimed his father king of Scotland. They might be amused at the inconsequence of the change of trades in Perth. Once it was tobacco and snuff and ropes and gloves that they worked at; the father of Scott's Fair Maid of Perth was a glover. Now it's whisky and insurance and glass. What will it be tomorrow? They would readily envisage a scene in the Carse where the new railway ran close to the Tay and a goods train overtook a sailing ship and hooted as it passed it and maybe the exasperated captain, seeing an ancient craft coming to the end of its days, shouted at the enginedriver, 'I hope yer biler bursts!'

In the sixties I spent twelve hours at Perth Railway Station, gathering information for a radio programme. Passengers and goods were on the move all the time. I had no idea that there were so many Scots who wanted to be some place else. Perth was the hub of the wheel of Scotland, in perpetual motion. Like shipping on the Tay, the railways offered not only a service to the public but a way of life to those engaged in their operation. In the early days of steam, the Perth enginedrivers spent part of their Sundays, unpaid, instructing the apprentices in running repairs, and initiating them, in the manner of their mediaeval masters, into their craft, its lore and prides, its kenspeckle characters and the heroic and more usually humorous events that befell them, the glories of the railway races from London to Aberdeen. There was a railway culture, a soil into which the apprentices put down roots and which nourished them and gave them a pride of identity. But it's what are called the human stories that rivet the attention of the young. An Aberdeen teenager, lodged in Perth Prison, told me that when his father, an enginedriver, was driving the Aberdeen-Glasgow train, and when he came within earshot of the prison, he sounded a pre-arranged whistle. For our Scottish teenagers that communication between father and son would hold more significance than an archive of royal Jameses.

1987   **Sir Nicholas Hardwick Fairbairn**

A Life Is Too Short

As was then my habit, I went to Perth races. My interest at race meetings, such as it is, is more in watching the fillies off the course compete with one another, rather than those on it. Hippolatry is not in my blood, gyniolatry is. My view of horse-racing rather coincides with that of the Shah of Persia, who on being invited by Her Majesty the Queen to attend the Derby stakes, replied 'No thank you, Ma'am. It is already well known to me that one horse can run faster than another.' So can one filly, but frequently hoping to be overtaken. In the evening on Tuesday and Thursday were held the two Perth balls. The second of them was the grander. It took place in the magnificent ballroom of the Perth Courthouse, with its supreme sprung floor, amid diamonds and sashes and chandeliers, and a good blend of conviviality, sensuality, formality and champagne. Nowadays there is only one ball instead of two, and with crass insensitivity it has been banished from the room which was built for it, so that the bureaucracy can turn it into offices. If, in Burkes great words, 'the age of chivalry' died in 1789, then the age of romance joined it on a bureaucratic scaffold one hundred and eighty-five years later.

Kenneth Roy

Travels In a Small Country

THE FLAGS were out in Perth. Pink blossom fluttered across the playgrounds of South Inch. On the other side of the river, baronial piles set among high trees brought to mind the merchant class which made its fortune here.

Perth is affluent but discreet. When visiting journalists come to report a conference and are required to inject a little local colour into the proceedings, they reach for the adjective *genteel* to describe the town's essential quality. Poor Perth: condemned by Fleet Street to everlasting gentility.

Even its Tourist Information place is superior: housed in a converted waterworks, no less. But the audio-visual entertainment sounded just the same as all the others. Somewhere in the nether regions, in a specially preserved tank of murky cliches, an Equity voice intoned the beauties of the surrounding area. 'In Perthshire, no day is long enough,' the voice said. Cue pipers.

Opposite the City Hall, the pipers had not arrived, but they would be here soon enough. Workmen shrouded in dust were putting down paving stones outside a new shopping centre, in preparation for the grand opening. Attached to a statue erected in memory of King Edward VII was a developer's sign: LAST FEW UNITS TO LET.

'Provost John Mathieson will open Grosvenor Developments' new 100,000 square feet St John's Centre, Perth, at 10.30am on Thursday,' reported the *Perthshire Advertiser* in its front page story. 'Early visitors will receive free carrier bags, car stickers and hand-outs from the St John's Centre promotional team and will be entertained by Scottish country dancing and military music.'

It was all happening. At the City Hall, they were getting ready for the local Festival of the Arts; at the new shopping centre, they were getting ready for Provost John Mathieson. I had half expected the town to be still recovering from the personal appearance of the Prime Minister, who had just launched her Election campaign at the Scottish Tory conference. But that was already old hat. I could find no trace of Conservative ladies with blue rinses or television executives sobering up in the City Mills Hotel. A new show was about to open – and hurry, hurry, there were only a few units still to let.

In the foyer of Perth Theatre, where morning coffee was being served, a young actress was sounding off on the subject of theatrical agents. At another table, a fat woman in her early thirties was conducting a monologue on religion.

'I said at the Bible study, I said to them – is the Pope going to Heaven? Nobody answered that. Nobody had the nerve to say he wasn't going to Heaven.'

The woman with her seemed puzzled.

'Why is he not going to Heaven?'

'Because he is not born again.'

'Oh!'

After this, her friend confined herself to nods and periodic murmurs of vague agreement.

I wandered over to the exhibition of photographs on the far wall and tried to work out what the Pope would have to do to get to Heaven. Become a Presbyterian perhaps? The pictures looked a bit odd.

'There are people,' she said, 'who by their works, not knowing about the Gospel, who by the purity of their works will go to Heaven. Because of what they are.'

That was a generous concession. But it was hard to say (for she did not elaborate) what kind of selfless activity might qualify for admission.

'It is not just the Pope. There are Church of Scotland people who do not know about being born again. I feel like saying, you lot are so narrow-minded, I feel like walking out, but then I say to myself that would be silly, really silly.'

Here on the far wall, the exhibition consisted of black and white photographs of teenage girls. Girls in school uniform, girls playing tennis, girls on the beach, girls in gym slips. Meanwhile, over at the Christian table, the talk was of sin.

'They all sin. They sin all the time. And yet they find it easy to have faith, easy to pray. But if you say you don't find it easy, they'll come down on you, oh yes they will.'

A few doors along, at the Granada TV rental shop, I was brought up by an extraordinary sight. Every set in the place, and there were twenty six sets, was tuned to the live transmissions from the General Assembly of the Church of Scotland.

The effect was mesmeric. When the camera cut away from the speaker, I caught twenty six identical images of Mr Bob Kernohan, Editor of Life and Work. Then we were given a shot of the Assembly voting. Whatever the motion was, it was carried overwhelmingly, for in every corner of the Granada TV rental shop, men in black suits rose to their feet in perfect unison. Next, the BBC showed us twenty six handlebar moustaches – these appeared to belong to the Moderator – followed by twenty six Reverend Duncan Bogles from Dumfries. Reverend Bogle preached a short sermon before giving way to a man wearing twenty six blue ties and twenty six matching hankies. According to the caption, this sartorially elegant figure was also a Reverend. Just under his twenty six chins, there was attached to the sets a sales bill with a curiously apt message: SUPER SAVERS.

The Bible Study woman in Perth Theatre would be disappointed by the deliberations of the General Assembly. The super savers of the Assembly are not the born-again evangelicals, whose occasional utterances are greeted with scarcely disguised embarrassment, but the low-key businessmen of Kirk headquarters with their latest plans for closing down uneconomic congregations. Every time the Assembly meets, another light goes out in a parish somewhere in Scotland.

Despite its diminished authority in the national life, the Church of Scotland continues to act as if the world outside is still listening. It declares periodically on such matters as unemployment (against) and devolution (for). And it is fond of asserting its old right to be a court of law. On these occasions, there is all the panoply of a criminal trial – dock, accused, counsel, verdict, sentence, the lot. The crime is not usually very exceptional – a minister gone barking mad, or off with the session clerk's wife – and the worst the Assembly can do is deprive a man of his living. But there is something not quite wholesome about the ritual of judgement by mass jury.

In search of a drink, I set off down a road marked CLOSED. A plate at the entrance told me this was Watergate, a place of some fashion and importance in medieval Perth. Nobles and gentry built town houses here, and cultivated gardens which extended to the banks of the Tay. James IV lived here, and Oliver Cromwell, when he held Perth, lodged in Watergate. What was left of it? I prepared an inventory:

ON THE LEFT:

Perth and Kinross District Council Headquarters; John Queen & Son (Plumbing and eating Engineer; itch & Bath oo Specialists); and the side entrance of a stark modern edifice out of which jogged two middle-aged men in shorts and teeshirts. I found to my dismay that this was the Perth office of the Inland Revenue.

ON THE RIGHT:

Fairways Business Services; a bicycle shed; The Windsor Function Suite; a few well-preserved examples of Scottish vernacular (houses probably, though it was difficult to tell their present use); and a pub called The Gowrie Hoose, commemorating a Perth conspiracy too obscure to recall.

Where might Jamie have slept? I fancied the *itc & Bath oo Specialists* as a possibility. Cromwell, on the other hand, would surely have preferred to lodge with the tax man.

There was no obvious reason why Watergate should be signposted CLOSED. Perhaps it was in mourning for glory days beyond recall.

Spurning the Gowrie Hoose, I gave my pre-lunchtime custom to the Salutation, which advertises itself as the oldest established hotel in Scotland (1699). Upstairs, the Rotary Club of St John was preparing to meet in a room next to the bar. An official sat at a table just inside the door, scoring off names of Members Attending.

I asked the barmaid for directions to St John's Church.

'St John's Kirk,' she corrected me. 'We aye cry it Kirk.'

'Kirk it is, then.'

'My daughter's gettin' married there next year. For weddings, you pay somebody a fiver and they'll ring the bells. Lovely when they ring the bells.'

'I'm sure...'

She laughed. 'Easy pleased, I am!'

I explained that I was going to St John's Kirk for the opening event of the Perth Festival. The barmaid said the festival was great, and getting better every year. But when I remarked on the flags, she said she doubted whether they were connected with that. More likely, she thought, the flags were up for the opening of the new shopping centre.

Personally, she didn't want the new shopping centre. It would only take trade away from the High Street. Already, two chain stores had decided to quit and relocate in the St John's Centre. What would happen to their old premises? What would happen to the High Street generally?

These were good questions, articulated by an ordinary citizen of Perth. I looked in vain for answers in the *Perthshire Advertiser*. The paper's front page story described Grosvenor Developments as 'one of the UK's leading specialists' - in what, it didn't say – and reported that they had been joined in partnership by Perth and Kinross District Council, Best (Estates) Ltd., and somebody improbably named G. Percy Trentham. It wasn't clear what part G. Percy Trentham played in the grand scheme, which according to the newspaper 'involved a three-phase development'. We were invited to turn to pages eight and nine to learn more. Pages eight and nine were devoted to an advertising feature in which contractors and sub-contractors indulged in an orgy of self-congratulation.

The accompanying text was unrestrained in its approval. 'Perth's most spectacular shopping sensation'. 'An exciting milestone in local retail trends'. 'A spacious and comfortable shopping environment'. As befitted their position as one of the UK's leading specialists, Grosvenor Developments had included glass-sided lifts; a spiral staircase; 'impressive water features'; and, of course, a multi-storey car park. 'No more struggling through snow or dodging the rain to get from one shop to another,' reported the *Advertiser*. 'The entire centre is covered.' (Hassle-free, as they say in Stirling). But from the barmaid in the Salutation Hotel, I had heard a very different story.

Is the St John's Centre really needed? The shops in and around the High Street seemed at first glance to offer anything that the people of Perth might conceivably want to buy. But for some reason, the impulse towards the destruction of traditional shopping streets and their replacement by monstrous indoor 'centres' is proving irresistable to local authorities.

The charming lady at the door of St John's Kirk assured me that there was no admission to the lunchtime concert, merely what she called a 'silver collection'.

'I hadn't realised there was a festival on,' I said.

'Shame on you. Well, you'll just have to come back next year, and stay for the whole ten days.'

'So what is it? A small version of Edinburgh?'

'Oh, much better than Edinburgh. Much more... (she searched

for the appropriate word) ...select.'

As I moved away, she added smilingly: 'Of course, we don't have the MONEY of Edinburgh!'

The Young Musicians' Lunchtime Concert by the pupils of Perth High School conjured up a vision of school choirs and brass bands. Instead, we were treated to a classical programme of short solo items performed by eight of the music department's brightest young stars.

St John's was founded by David I in 1126. It was here, according to tradition, that Edward III murdered his brother, the Earl of Cornwall, in 1335; here, too, that John Knox preached a sermon notably provocative even by his inflammatory standards. After eight hundred years of blood and thunder, the old kirk now resounded to nothing more threatening than the bassoon, and the accordion, and Allan Smith's exquisitely played violin; and a congregation of Perth mums and dads, and senior girl groupies, and I sat compelled and moved by the experience.

It was half past one when the concert ended. Too late to go hunting for somewhere decent to eat, so across the street to a dreary, poorly lit restaurant. Very quiet, but it was one of these places where the waitresses are always absorbed in resetting tables and the customer is made to feel invisible.

At the next table, a girl of about twenty, as small and pretty as H. V. Morton's prototype of a Perth maiden, was talking to a friend about her forthcoming wedding. What she would like to do, she said, was hire the City Hall and invite three hundred guests. Her pal was not so sure about big weddings. She had been married in the registry office and held her reception in Pizzaland.

'Look at Julie. Had five hundred guests at her wedding. Now she's divorced.'

'What a shame,' said the bride-to-be.

'And they only got wed three years ago.'

Julie and her husband had separated after a few months. The man had been totally possessive, set in his ways, wouldn't allow her to buy anything, do anything, without asking.

Listening to this story, the bride-to-be turned pensive. Her face showed that Julie's tragedy had struck a tendon of doubt somewhere, enough to cloud a young girl's dream of enchantment. It was a question of growing up, she said. And sometimes she felt that her boyfriend had done all his growing up, whereas she had a lot of growing up still to do. Her friend said nothing, and the mood lightened again. Soon, the two of them were asking to see the 'function suite', where the real reception would take place, rather than the idealised version that would never be.

They skipped upstairs, and the echo of their light, warm laughter slowly faded.

1988   **Ian Wallace**

Reflections on Scotland

IF THERE HAD been a prize for the most attractively designed waterworks in Britain in the last century Perth would have been up with the leaders, if not the outright winner. It was necessary to build it near the River Tay in an area of fine buildings, and the local councillors were determined that the new amenity should be in keeping with its surroundings. They had the right man in charge for that. Dr Adam Anderson, a noted academic, not only devised the scheme to draw water from the Tay, filter it and pump it into a reservoir in the top of the building – he designed the building as well. This rotunda in classical style is still an ornament to the city 160 years later, and now does duty as the tourist information centre. One of Dr Anderson's most delightful touches was the Grecian urn to round off the steam engine's chimney. The present one is a fibreglass replica of the original, and indeed the whole building was extensively restored in the early 1970s. Soon after it was completed in 1834, Dr Anderson wrote in chalk over the door, 'Aquam Igne et Aqua Haurio' - I draw water by fire and water, the words are still there, not in chalk, but in letters of gold. Dr Anderson deserved many gold sovereigns for his efforts. He only received 315, and his letter of complaint remained unanswered three years after it was sent.

As a keen spectator of many sports, cricket among them, I know how easy it is to make inaccurate statements, liable to be instantly challenged by a battery of better informed experts; but I'm reasonably confident in suggesting that, indirectly, Napoleon was responsible for the first cricket to be played on the North Inch at Perth. Some of the French prisoners from the Napoleonic Wars were housed in Perth Gaol, which was originally built to house them in 1812. Their guards included a regiment of Hussars, one of whose summer recreations was cricket, and they chose the North Inch, which was ideal for the purpose – and still is today. It's reported that the Hussars had no difficulty in interesting the young men of Perth in the game. After such auspicious beginnings, it's no surprise that Perth Cricket Club is one of the finest in Scotland. As golf was played on the North Inch for hundreds of years before the Hussars arrived, it would be interesting to know how many of them returned south with a proficiency in the royal and ancient game to match their leg breaks and cover drives.

1993   **Geoff Brown**

The River Tay and Its People

I WAS BORN in the Barnhill part of Perth and am a real native of this area. I moved to Glencarse in the Carse of Gowrie in 1971. I live in a house close to my builder's yard between the river and the railway line, a very pleasant location from which to work. I used to fish on the river as a boy but between my business and St Johnstone, I don't have enough time these days.

I took charge at St Johnstone in 1986 and there have been a lot of changes since then. I have supported the team since I was a lad and it was really a great opportunity for me. My investment in the club has been more in time than in money, because we were able to sell the previous site at Muirton Park. But it has been hard work. I would say that running a football club is in many ways the same as running a business: both require leadership and the ability to work as a team. If you treat people the way you expect to be treated and work well together, there is no end to the success you can achieve.

I believe that in McDiarmid Park we have one of the most advanced stadia in the country. The new stadium has had a knock-on effect on the quality of the football and is an important addition to the community which can be used by local people. It annoys me when people go on about Ibrox. When Rangers chairman David Murray said to me that we were two of the most forward-thinking clubs in the country, I replied that the honour belonged to St Johnstone alone because our stadium is completely new, while his is second-hand!

McDiarmid Park is the only stadium in Britain to fully comply with the Taylor report; we moved here in July 1989 just three months after the Hillsborough tragedy which led to the Taylor recommendations. At the end of last season all we had to do was reseed the pitch and test 25 per cent of the crush barriers and that was it. Every other ground had to do much more. I would say that Perth has undergone a real transformation in the last few years and it is now definitely a city of the 1990's. I am pleased that St Johnstone has been part of the transformation.

*   *   *

1993   Ann Gloag

The River Tay and Its People

I HAVE LIVED in Perth all my life. Before we started Stagecoach I worked in Bridge of Earn Hospital as a theatre sister. I would never live anywhere other than Perth but I admit I am biased. With its river setting, the city is very picturesque and is well provided for with its theatre and leisure facilities. Our group headquarters is based in Perth and the location has no disadvantage for an international operation at all. It is extremely convenient for airports and is basically a lovely place to live. I suppose I really should walk by the Tay and take advantage of the area's beautiful scenery but when I've been travelling all week my favourite thing is to sit back and enjoy the company of my family at home. I look forward to the day when I will actually be able to enjoy this area to the full.

1993   Provost Jean McCormack

The River Tay and Its People

PERTH HAS UNDERGONE a major transformation in the last few years and, through initiatives such as the Perth Partnership, which draws together the private and public sectors, and Perth in Bloom, we have made great efforts to ensure that the city looks its best. Apart from the pedestrianisation of the High Street and the changes in the commercial part of the city, we have greatly improved Perth's parks. On the banks of the river we have opened up an old walkway leading to the Rodney Pavilion and park. The next upgrading we are considering is widening the pavements of Tay Street and creating a boulevard-style atmosphere. In fact, Perth achieves a Parisian feel already, especially in May when artists display their works on the riverside railings.

The Tay is one of Perth's most important tourist attractions. We are considering reintroducing Black Swans on the river. The original Black Swans were gifted by our twin town of Perth, Australia, but they disappeared. The council chambers have a balcony looking out over the river and people find it very relaxing to walk there after a tense debate. The river has a calming influence. I come from Dundee originally and have always been very close to the river.

1993   Graham Ogilvy

The River Tay and Its People

SEEMINGLY IMPERVIOUS to the weary grind of recession and depression, Perth has emerged over the last decade as a confident commercial and tourism centre, strong in identity and sure in purpose. Not for Perth the fading dowdiness of a tweedy county town which loomed so large less than 20 years ago. The Fair City has built on its strengths and avoided resting on its laurels.

The contrast with Perth's larger neighbour to the east could not be more striking. In the Tay's tale of two cities the gap between prospering Perth and struggling Dundee seems destined to widen: where Dundee has yet to succeed, Perth has triumphed; while Dundee's population declines, Perth's rises; and while Dundee wrestles with its apparently intractable identity crisis, Perth gets down to business, emerging as an attractive location for corporate headquarters.

A significant element of Perth's easy self-confidence and prosperity derives from its strong sense of identity and purpose. Always a strategic crossroads, Perth was Scotland's capital until 1482 when James III transferred the seat of government to Edinburgh. It's location at the mouth of the Tay valley made it a natural gateway to the Highlands, a factor recognised as early as AD 80 when the Romans, led by Agricola, built a fort at a crossing place near the Tay's confluence with the Almond and named it Bertha – from which the city takes its modern name.

1994 Campbell Steven

Enjoying Perthshire

A NECESSARY JOURNEY to Perth on 2nd May gave us the chance of one of our traditional forays on the North Inch beside the Tay. A county cricket match in progress gave an added touch of summer to a day of pleasantly warm sun-blinks. The Tay itself, with a flickering of sand martins and mallards in plenty (nine ducklings in one family party) had an unusually benevolent look about it. Several merganser pairs and a solitary goosander drake with three redheads in attendance were enjoying their feeding close under the further bank, while the familiar guano-white roosting tree (at that time still standing) had its quota of cormorant tenants, perched like a gang of scrawny vultures hungry for carrion.

1995 Jack Webster

Back in Bloom (from *The Herald*)

THE PAST FEW YEARS have seen one of those curious transformations which can bring the spotlight on a community before there is time to analyse what actually happened. In that time, Perth has emerged from its traditional image of the douce county town to become the flavour of the age among Scottish towns and cities, dynamic and progressive. Is it all a coincidence? Or the outcome of shrewd and deliberate policy?

In the heart of the town you come upon the impressive kirk of St John's. The Rev David Ogston, confirms the new confidence he has seen developing in Perth. 'It faced a choice between change and the genteel resignation of fading into a nonentity of a place. Thankfully, successive councils and provosts showed initiative, bravado, imagination and energy and took up the attitude of "let's do it!" Now there is a new feeling of self-awareness and a general buoyancy.'

You wander through the neat streets of this prosperous town and absorb more than a hint of what is currently called the feel-good factor. Alongside the modern temples of consumer worship there are, happily, still shops which look as if they have served the community for a long time and with quality and service.

1996 Magnus Magnusson

Heritage of Perth

SO MUCH of Scotland's history is woven into the story of Perth. It was, after all, the capital city at one point in its history. To many, Perth is a city to pass through on the way north or south: but it would be in the traveller's best interest to stay awhile and explore the Perth of today as well as Perth of yesteryear.

The Fair City remains in our minds as one of our most delightful places – a gateway not only to the Highlands but to Scotland itself.

1997 Maggie Lennon

Small Country: Ten Years of the Scottish Review 1995-2004

NEXT, PERTH.
Fiona has a problem with Perth.
She works, temporarily it is to be hoped, for the prison service

and finds Perth prison threatening and unpleasant with good reason. Although I wanted to see it, I said I'd settle for the outside. I could picture the tiny Alice in Wonderland door set in the huge gate, out of which released prisoners were ejected with all their worldly possessions tied up in a brown paper bundle.

I was sorely disappointed. There was no tiny wee door – instead, a solid wooden gate surrounded by high security locks, which looked unlikely to open this side of Doomsday. Fiona confirmed a few days later that the brown paper bundles tied up with string are a thing of the past too.

Prisons used to be about correction and punishment, then they were about rehabilitation and improvement. Looking at the formidable entrance to Perth, I realised that what they are really about is keeping two sides of society away from each other and maintaining that divide.

But there is more to Perth than the prison. There are shops, lots of them, and a silly one-way system to keep you from them. The centre is pedestrianised and replete with bronze statues, including the town's own Fair Maid. An early morning drunk was talking to her, possibly for want of more serious discourse from the locals.

Perth High Street has the same chain stores as anywhere else, though ten days before Christmas they were eerily quiet. Where was everyone? Not at church, I was pretty sure. Eventually we found them in the local Argos, filling out their order forms as if they were lottery tickets. This was shopping of a kind, but shopping by numbers – an easy, let-someone-else-do-all-the-work method of purchasing that requires little effort and even less imagination.

In search of a more traditional shopping experience, we went to Wm. Watson and Son, a fancy goods shop and shrine to Royal Doulton, with cosies of novelty tea pots and litters of china puppies. Like many of the family businesses in the side streets, Wm. Watson and Son saw no need to cheapen the sabbath by trading. But even if they had been open, who was going to pay £190 for a group of china-nesting penguin chicks.

There were more penguins in the main shopping centre keeping Santa's grotto company. One nodded his head disconsolately, another spun round and round on one foot, listing dangerously. The festive scene was rounded off by a jolly eskimo who lurched from side to side and whose complexion bore the hallmarks of a heavy drinker. Of Santa himself there was no sign; nor were there any children waiting to sit on a fat old stranger's lap. For kids whose Christmas is supplied courtesy of Father Argos, Santa probably seems passe.

Though perhaps not as passe as the local pantomime, *Sinbad the Sailor*, whose billing as a traditional family entertainment might have been a dig at the glossier vehicles of the cities. It promised a chorus from the local dance school, lots of cross dressing, and a cast of enthusiastic unheard-ofs. The rest of Perth Theatre's winter repertoire was hardly more inspiring – a tired provincial diet of farce, musical comedy, George Bernard Shaw, and a John Godber offering called *Lucky Sods*, supposedly a parable of our times about the perils of winning the lottery. This theatre in the heart of Scotland couldn't muster a Scottish play, not even the Scottish play.

As we returned to the car past walking Argos bags, we saw a store called Hope. It was shut.

But the road and the miles to Dundee lay ahead, and I had promised Fiona a treat.

Neither of us had a problem with this.

Fifteen minutes later, we arrived at a celebrated landmark on the Perth to Dundee road: the Horn Milk Bar. As a child, a visit to the Horn was the highlight of a run in the car. It was little more than a caravan in those days, but with a giant draught board on which the pieces were moved around by boat hooks. Now it advertises itself as a 'caff', complete with gift shop and takeaway cake board. You could smell the tablet from the car park.

Colin Gibson

Nature Diary (from *The Courier*)

MAKING FOR PERTH, I never followed the road below the 'ire hill' of Kinnoull without gazing up in wonder at that great crag that lifts its 'face o' stone', as the poet William Soutar called it, above the tidal flow of the Tay.

It rises to 720 feet above the river, and on its crest stands a ruined watchtower. An interesting structure, but it was never anything else but a ruin and an imitation.

It was, in fact, built by a long-departed laird – the 9th Earl of Kinnoull, who had an eye for romantic scenery and an admiration for the Rhine and its baronial castles as well as for his native Tay.

This gentleman also had a stone table placed on the hilltop. He was so fond of the view that he often lunched there al fresco. But no doubt that was in the summer when the sky was blue and the sun shone.

When last I was on Kinnoull a cold northeaster sobbed and girned in the corrie called 'Windy Ghoul', and patches of snow lay around the cave known since the 6th century as the 'Dragon's Den.' It was here, according to tradition, that the Pictish King Brude slew a monster-beast – this as a token of his esteem for St Serf, whose sacred life had deeply impressed him.

That day, I went down by Corsiehill – at one time a picturesque clachan. In 1787 Robert Burns halted there on his way to Perth by the Braes Road, and he was thrilled by the fine vista opening out before him.

But before leaving the skyline of Kinnoull, I tried to find the place from which it is said you can rouse a clear echo from the rocks. Despite much calling and hallooing, however, I didn't find it. But I suddenly noticed that a number of visitors had stopped, obviously wondering why the man was standing there bawling away for no apparent reason.

I hastily departed.

Michael W. Russell

In Waiting – Travels in the Shadow of Edwin Muir

I AM VERY FOND of Perth and was even before I spent five weeks here in the run up to the constituency by-election in 1995. It is a pity that Muir devotes only one line to it - 'I stopped in Perth to buy a basket of strawberries and pushed on to a remote part of Angus where I wished to see a married couple, old friends of mine, who were running a farm there"– as to me it is one of the most Scottish of towns, and yet also one of the most modern. Like all Scottish towns it has simply grown – so driving in is a patchwork experience, moving past modern estates to Edwardian villas and on to car showrooms, tyre depots and then into the town centre itself.

Perth sits comfortably on the River Tay, and the best of the centre also abuts onto the river itself, with traffic guided over two bridges, which are (unusually) the boundaries of the city. Perth is a city, and calls itself such – with some justification as it is the fastest-growing conurbation in Scotland, and will, in size, overtake Dundee early in the next century. It has already overtaken Dundee in attraction.

There is little in the centre that is really old – or at least looks that way, apart from St John's Kirk, which is the cradle of the Scottish Reformation. The impressive City Chambers look late–18th century, tarted up a bit in the next century, but they sit cheek by jowl with shops and offices, and with a wealth of pubs and restaurants that make the city a good place to spend an evening. Such an integration of civic activity and service is just the right note to strike.

Perth is also rich in hotels, my favourite being the Salutation – though its claim to be the oldest hotel in Scotland is probably bogus. None the less, and despite the ravages of the all-purpose modern hotel interior designer, it has a comfortable and antique feel, with a splendid window in the first floor dining room that gives a view of a single city street that speaks volumes about the place. And it certainly did play host to Charles Edward Stuart during his triumphal sweep down Scotland in 1745 – a sweep that was exceeded in speed only by his retreat the following year!

Modernism has made the main shopping thoroughfare as bland as anywhere else in Scotland – there is even an indoor mall – yet the streets constantly surprise, producing small faded cafes, and strange shops dedicated to odd fashions or pursuits in every nook and cranny. Even the straight and ordered part of the centre – slightly grim with its severe tenements – has a variety that is hard to find elsewhere.

Perth is also prosperous – an Aga dealership gives testimony to the wealth of the surrounding countryside, as does a Laura Ashley outlet. But its community spirit means that the Perth Theatre lies almost next to that imported centre of home counties good taste, and round the corner one can hire a kilt from an old-fashioned tailor that looks (and is) planted in the last century. Perth City Halls lie at the heart of the city and although they are too small now for the type of political conference that is the norm, there has been an attempt to make them more attractive by sprinkling pavement cafes around. Inside the wood-panelled splendour has been restored and the gold leaf re-gilded: only the massive organ sits mute, waiting for someone knowledgeable enough to make its sound fill the building.

Perhaps I like Perth because I associate it with success: it was here that Alex Salmond became SNP leader in 1990, and at the same time, as his campaign manager, I avoided being defeated for the party office I held. I spent the only sleepless night of my life before that vote, working out in my head again and again whether we had really done things the right way, and if so was there any possibility of defeat. My head said no, but my usual caution said, 'Of course... anything can happen.' And in 1995 I ran the campaign that won the by-election – again saying to myself for days before that we must win because no one else could, yet constantly questioning whether the right things were taking place, and whether the right campaign was being run. But I also associate Perth with long evenings and pleasant dinners, good company and dry weather and a sense of wellbeing enhanced by the surroundings and the people.

There is no doubt that this eastern part of Scotland (we are only 20 miles or so from the sea) is drier and the ambient weather better than the west where I live and where I was brought up. That fact seems to be reflected in the bustle and style of the city – less hiding from the rain and the wind, and more openness and casual conversation. Perhaps I am imagining it, but the strong voices of the farmers and their wives greeting each other in the open streets is a sound I don't associate with Oban or Fort William: there the conversation is more intimate, the gatherings more huddled.

Tonight I am having dinner with work colleagues, preparing for a special party conference. Out of the richness of choice we select a Thai restaurant (I have been there before with the BBC) and we have an excellent meal, though the table keeps expanding as more people turn up, and the nervous waiter is beginning to have a breakdown as his work expands also. The talk revolves in small groups, occasionally widening to embrace the whole table, the falling apart again into twos and threes. Inevitably it is about what we share – the minutiae of the moment, of polls and problems, and possibilities ahead. This is not a unique event: any group of people who work together know the syndrome, and know that it is a fragile covering of common experiences that lies over the vast deep of personal lives, ambitions, histories and futures.

Eventually we pay, and walk out into an early summer street that is still bright with the reflected light of northern hemisphere evenings. There are shafts of sunlight lying along the road, spilling into the town from the surrounding hills. A couple of us walk to the river, which is rolling and surging towards the sea, but controlled and quiet in this season, glassy on its top in the calm air.

Much later I am ensconced in MP Roseanna Cunningham's

office, reacting to a new poll and coming to terms with the fact that to the younger members of our staff the confidence and self-assertion of Scottish voters is not a surprise, but an inevitability. They are confident – with the confidence of youth – that the future does belong to them, and that such a future will be better, more open and more generous than the age in which they grew up.

For me, that hope is summed up in a place like Perth. An ancient city, it has taken part in many of the major events of our history, yet has gone on growing and developing and being renewed. It took the Union in its stride, and it can take a new future just as well. To the outside it may seem quiet and conservative. But it has a will and a spirit of its own. It wants to be part of the world, and it will make it on its own terms.

The river keeps on running to the sea. The town keeps on growing. And the people keep on living here, welcoming new blood and enlisting them in the quiet, determined, civilised, cause of the city.

1999 David W. McFadden

An Innocent in Scotland

THE PROUD CITY of Perth (often pronounced *Pairth*) is an odd place for the Isle of Skye Hotel, but there it is. It's a handsome big structure too, and one would suppose that they might have a Perth Hotel on the remote Isle of Skye itself. The Iona Hotel, much smaller of course, is also here. One might surmise that Perth has traditionally been a stopping-off place for English tourists rushing up to the Western Isles, except of course for the fact that it's not really en route. But one could not imagine a lovlier town, and all the little old ladies are ravishingly dressed as they sashay their way to church on this warm and sunny Sunday morn, their husbands being at home with Sunday-morning flu.

The Inner Ring is the oldest part of the city, and at first glance there seem to be Greek temples all over the place. The Perth Sheriff Court House looks like a Greek temple, as does the City Water Works which was built in 1832 and has been transformed into the Ferguson Gallery, with an ugly sculpture of a naked geometric woman out front. The sculpture has no curves, just angles. There's a lot of that around Scotland – as if curves were of the devil, and angles of the angels.

There were great tragedies in this town in the storied past, for sure. A lot of people were burned to death here for such things as sorcery, dancing on Sundays, and playing cards one minute after midnight Saturday night. As I think these ugly thoughts, a stiff, hot wind comes up from the southwest and almost blows me away. *'When you're here,'* says Mr Morton*, *'never for one minute can you feel unconscious of the wildness which lies beyond the gates of Perth … you walk through grey-stone streets, modern, but still, in their skyline and their grim bulk they recall a more ancient Perth, and you smell a wind that comes sweet over miles of desolate heather'.*

I don't know about that, but two ducks and a tennis ball are floating by on the River Tay, spanned by an old bridge with its seven round arches, any one of which is large enough to coast through on a beer barge. I feel a terrible stranger in Perth. People glance at me, then glance away quickly, wondering if there's anything they could do to hasten me on my way.

Mr Morton, there are some interesting-looking people around this town, but the hordes of *'small, pretty girls'* you raved about (*'Perth, like Gloucester, where matches are made – this is no pun – is full of small, pretty girls'*) seem to have lived their lives out and died. You described Perth as being *'as Scottish as a plate of cockaleekie or a warm bannock'*, and that's pretty darned Scottish if you ask me. Also you climbed that hill over there, and came back with a terrific line for your book: *'I climbed Kinnoul Hill before breakfast.'* You mention Bob Andrews, a famed golfer from Perth *'who could drive a ball off the face of a gold watch without damaging it.'* And you have a refreshing comment on a young fellow who wants to be a farmer when he grows up: *'What a refreshing lad! No engines in his soul!'* When I was a kid there were scads of old-timers with Mortonesque senses of humour. Reading Morton resurrects them for me.

A small yellow bus goes by, taking people to the REFORMED BAPTIST CHURCH, a miserable face in each window. They look as if they're suffering from too much moral superiority. As the Scots themselves say (but not these Scots), 'One can die of too little whisky.' Right in front of a bakery shop on High Street there's a man cheekily putting his hand all the way up his girlfriend's skirt, and on a Sunday morning, too. He also seems to be probing her ear with the tip of his twitching tongue. Maybe the Reformed Baptists looked so miserable because their eyes had offended them as they passed by these horny devils.

I'd like to pop into this little bakery with a rather unusual sign out front, reading MCSORLEY'S MORNING ROLLS ARE FAMED MORNING ROLLS. But the store's closed for the day. And then there's Mrs McIntyre, obviously a thorn in Mr McSorley's side, for her morning rolls are not only famed but have also been written about by top authors such as Peter Irving, who is quoted, shamelessly, right in the window, as having written, with an imitative tautology perhaps: MRS MCINTYRE'S MORNING ROLLS ARE THE BEST ROLLS IN SCOTLAND, IN SCOTLAND THE BEST. Not one of the best, but the actual best. Take that, McSorley. And, tsk, even the fish-and-chip shop, with a sign in the window saying WE FRY IN VEGETABLE OIL, is closed. They must have been playing hooky the day they studied transitive and intransitive verbs. Even the galleries and museums are closed.

Perth has wonderful footpaths and nature trails signposted right through town, historical walks, cultural walks, nature walks, walks along the canal, walks along the river, and it's a glorious town for walking all around, even for people who use Perth as a starting point for more ambitious cross-country walks. What better criterion is there for a city or a town or any place you want to live than it can be seen as a good place for walking, and will probably continue to be long after you can't walk any more!

On entering the vast regal gardens surrounding Scone Palace, two miles north of Perth, there's a sign saying MIND THE JACOB'S LAMBS – but there don't seem to be any lambs at all, though there are plenty of cows grazing away among the giant oak trees and serene peacocks. Scone Palace is a vast Victorian country home, very pleasing to the eye, and it's adjacent to the sacred site of Scone Abbey, in which kings from Kenneth II to James VI were crowned. You don't have to be Morton to feel in the air, and in the pricklings of your skin, that numerous wondrous and legendary things happened around here in days of yore.

Elspeth, the gap-toothed seductress at the ticket gate, doesn't mind stating unequivocally that she doesn't know the difference between a palace and a castle, but as for bars and pubs, she thought that bars might be a tad more expensive. (Why couldn't that fellow in the 'bar' in Kilmarnock have told me that?) We're surrounded by peacocks, but they don't seem to be of the familiar yappy, screeching variety: perhaps they've been trained with royal jolts of electricity only to wail when they absolutely must, so as not to deter tourists from buying tickets.

The occasional tourist bus features a driver behind the wheel reading a golf magazine, taking a break while merry holidayers elbow their way through the palace. Elspeth has a dangerous look in her eye.

'And the palace is actually open on Sundays?' I say, amazed.

'Oh yes,' she says, 'we're heathens around here.'

'I'm not surprised. You have that look about you.'

'Oh yes, when I was young I told the minister I didn't think one had to go to church to believe in God, and he told me I was heathen.' She pouted appealingly.

'If the minister said that, you must be, because they oughta know.'

'And I haven't been to church since.'

'Naturally you haven't.'

'And the funny thing is, the minister still comes to tea every Sunday.'

'That is strange. Probably a tribute to your excellent tea.'

'Yes, in this country if you make good tea it doesn't matter if you're Presbyterian or heathen.' She smiled broadly, then added that, coincidentally, she was named Elspeth after a famous witch from Dundee.

'And you yourself, would you be a witch?'

The eye contact was like a stick of dynamite.

'You'll have to find out yourself, won't you?'

In the palace, ropes guide the tourists along and discourage them from touching things. Tall, aristocratic-looking ladies, semi-literate but well-versed, dressed splendidly in the tartan of the family, but without the vulgar name tags of the lower classes, chat amiably with the tourists, though not without a whiff of condescension. One can imagine that, as the tourist load increases, the amiabilty will decrease.

One such woman tells me the eighth Earl of Mansfield lives here. Good guy? Yes, but he's just retired. He was a barrister by profession, in London, but when he was made earl, he came back to live in the family home. 'He's at the moment sitting in the garden.'

'I thought I saw some lazy bastard out there.'

'He's no bastard, but he is a bit lazy these days, because we haven't got barristers in Scotland, so he couldn't carry on with his accustomed rigour in his profession. He would have to become an advocate, which is the equivalent of a barrister.' I told her I understood perfectly.

The tourists move on, and we continue chatting. 'I hear they're having trouble with the lairds up there in Sutherland.'

'That all depends who you've met. I know the one they're having trouble with, and he's really a nice guy. You can't help what your forefathers did, can you? He is really a good laird, if you mean the one from Dunrobin Castle. Is that the one?'

'Yes. Lord. Lord...'

'Lord Melancholy,' she seemed to say, but that can't be right. 'Could not be a nicer guy – and he's done everything possible. But he's hated all the time. This chap was in the Metropolitan Police, you know, and he's an aristocrat. He's absolutely switched on to everything that's going on today and everything else too, he's not old, he's in his early forties, and absolutely the most capable person you could meet, and doing the best for everybody. There's always a few wild cards who cause a lot of trouble.'

She says the problem is simply that the lairds insist people get working harder. And they want to open their castles to the public.

'You can't fund an estate unless you open it for the public.'

'Mind you, they also complain about the Saudi Arabian lairds –'

'Oh, the Saudi Arabians are different. Somebody like Lord Melancholy – that's what it sounded like – 'is on every committee for keeping Scotland green. he's on every conservation programme known to mankind, he is the most up-to-the-minute chap you could ever meet, and I've met him personally very often and I can tell you he doesn't deserve any of the bad publicity he gets now and then. And the Saudis, I mean, who wants them anyway? Who wants that sort of money? It's very tainted. Oh, good afternoon, I mean good morning...'

Saved by a new bunch of tourists.

Back at the gatehouse, Elspeth is now revealing her political convictions. When I ask if Perth is a bit of a stronghold for Scottish Nationalism, she says: 'Everywhere, it''s everywhere in Scotland;

everybody resents England. We hate the BBC, for instance, because it's always 'we' when they mean England and England only, instead of 'we' when they mean the U.K., like when they're talking about the English football team it's always 'we', but when they're talking about the Scottish team it's always 'they'. This is infuriating and it gets everybody all riled up.' She is speaking calmly, but is giving the impression she is the sort who gets infuriated easily, and would come after you with a poleaxe if, for example, your puppy peed on her petunias. It sounds as if she wouldn't take kindly to any Scot who wasn't annoyed by such ethnic slurs on the part of the BBC.

*Mr Morton is the writer H. V. Morton. The quotations by David W. McFadden are from Morton's In Search of Scotland and appear in this book under the year 1929.

* * *

THE
Twenty-first Century

Perth Concert Hall

2002 **Brian Cox**

A Sense of Belonging To Scotland

IT WAS JUST BEFORE my eight birthday and the beginning of the summer. I remember my dad, my mum and my brother-in-law Dave going to Kinnoull, climbing up past the Cistercian Monastery up to the Folly. It had intrigued me ever since I was a baby when I used to go to Glasgow by car and see this lonely keep standing sentinel over the Tay Valley. Of course I didn't know then that this was a folly and had been designed as a homage to the Rhine.

I can still physically feel it so strongly that when my dad and I came up to Kinnoull, there was a very narrow ledge across to the Folly, which I was a little fearful of. My dad slung me on his back and, closing my eyes, he took across the ledge to the folly. There we sat, eating sandwich spread sandwiches with bits of cheddar cheese, and gazing at the Tay Valley. I remember that my father was wearing a sleeveless, fawn-coloured pullover, and I had these tweed shorts on which used to chafe my inner thighs. My dad was so transfixed by the view that we just sat there in wonderment. We were alone so I don't know what happened to the rest of the party. I remember a great sense of literally being above it all and my dad said to me: 'You'll never see a finer view in your life, Brian.' I think this was the last private moment my father and I ever spent together, because within a year he was dead.

Kinnoull is about texture, smell and intimacy. Whenever I see Kinnoull Hill from the Perth Road, it is 100% associated with my dad and I always feel that his spirit is there watching, waiting for me to come home.

*   *   *

2003   Quintin Jardine

Fallen Gods

THE PEOPLE ON THE NORTH INCH of Perth knew what was coming; many of them had experienced it before, and had supposed it could not happen again, even though in their heart of hearts they knew that it could.

A few piled sandbags in their doorways as high as they could, in the vain hope that they would prove an effective dam against the murky rushing water. The rest, those who had learned the hard lesson, moved as much of their furniture and as many of their valuables as they could into the upper floors of their terraced houses, and moved out to camp with relatives until the worst was over.

If they had stayed, they would have seen the river rise, little by little at first, then more swiftly, foot by foot, until finally it broke out, forming a new loch as it swept across the low-lying Inch, finding the streets and the waiting houses, making a mockery of the sandbags as it poured through them, finding the lower floors and cellars, and filling them to drowning depth.

Some had stayed, sitting safe upstairs, watching the personal disasters unfold, and shaking their heads as they did. 'This will never be allowed to happen again,' the politicians had declared as the North Inch householders had cleared away the mud from the last inundation.

But all too often, the attention span of politicians lasts no longer than the next election, and so, inevitably, it had.

2007   Iain Banks

The Steep Approach to Garbadale

ALL OF WHICH does kind of raise the question in Fielding's mind, What the hell am I doing here? as he drives into this scummy-looking housing estate in Perth. This is Perth, Scotland, we're talking about here, not Perth, Australia. Perth, Australia, is a beautiful, bright, sunny kind of place sprawling between the desert and the ocean – lots of surf and sizzling barbies and gleaming bronzed bodies. Perth, Scotland, is smaller and a lot less high-rise, sitting surrounded by low hills, forests and farmland. It boasts a variety of nice buildings and some very attractive detached properties facing the river, but not a lot of bronzed bodies that Fielding can see. He knows Scotland a bit – various family members have chosen to reside here for reasons best known to themselves and the Wopulds still, for now, have one of those vast huntin', shootin' 'n' fishin' estates in the far north of the place – but this is the first time he's been to Perth, he's fairly sure. The Fair City they call it, apparently. And its okay, he supposes, if you like old stuff and history and that sort of thing. He always had the impression that it was pretty posh and full of people wearing corduroy, tweeds and Barbour jackets, but this housing scheme on the outskirts looks like Chav City, Ned Central – a sink estate at the bottom of the U-bend.

...the whole scheme is nothing but islands – between long blocks of three and four storey flats covered in patchy pebble-dash spotted with poor-quality graffiti. The tiny gardens at the front of the flats are just plain unkempt. He's used to kempt.

There's a lot of litter about, some of it flying in the breeze coming funnelling down the street from the bright September clouds. He hasn't seen any bottles of Buckfast lying in the gutters – or any people lying in the gutter for that matter – and the kerb is lined with cars rather than wrecks, but – well – still.

Okay, some shops here, doors open but windows covered in metal grilles even now, during the day. Couple of thin, pimply youths standing outside something called Costcutter, sharing a bottle and watching the car slide past. *Yeah, it's an S-class 500 AMG, boyz. Look upon it and weep. See what you might get if you do your homework and work hard.*

2008 **Jeremy Duncan**

Perth: A Century of Change – The Fair City 1900–2000

MOST PEOPLE who do more than just pass through will have their own opinions on the city. These can range from a single person's view that it is 'a very married place' to those of a disaffected youth whose comment could be rephrased as 'not much goes on here.' On the other hand the elderly might say that it is an excellent place to retire to, central and neither too big nor too small, and parents might say that with its good schools and sporting and cultural facilities it is a fine place to bring up a family. As for the inhabitants, though, opinions are less positive. Even Onlooker, the Perthshire Advertiser columnist with a Biblical turn of phrase, stated in 1922 that 'Perthites are a strange people who taketh not well to strangers, and who looketh upon them, yea even with the eyes of suspicion from the toe to the crown of the head.' Perhaps he was thinking of the time in 1906 when German gypsies, in an act of mediaeval vindictiveness, were driven out of the city by a group of townspeople. He added that 'Perthites are a jealous people who do watch their neighbours carefully and are much learned in their affairs.' Things were no better 30 years later when that same newspaper described Perth folk as 'suspicious', stand-offish', 'snobbish', 'smug' and 'frostily indifferent' before modifying those less than flattering terms into a people 'minding their own business', 'living and letting live' and being 'courteous and incurious.' They took a decided turn for the worse in 1971 when the Courier and Advertiser published the following comments from a young man who had been in the city for over two years: 'Perth people take a great pride in their Fair City but they couldn't care less about newcomers. Married couples who have settled in the city take ages before they are accepted and this clannishness affects even their young families. The one good thing about Perth is that it is a fine place for passing through. And I am leaving it for good, I hope, next week.' Much, though, depends on one's personal outlook, and there are doubtless many incomers who regard Perth as a welcoming and friendly city.

Perth people were also inclined to take the law into their own hands. Prone to violence though they may have been, Perth people have also been surprisingly prudish. In 1972 the performance at the Sally of Cuddly Kim, described as an exotic dancer, was cancelled after protests from the public, and the following year topless dancer Angie suffered the same experience when the licensee at The Plough gave in to police pressure. As recently as 1989 a Perth newsagent was on trial for selling top-shelf soft porn, and the *Sunday Sport* was reported to the Advertising Standards Authority for putting up what some Perth folk considered to be offensive posters. Even the window displays in the Ann Summers shop were a bit too racy for some.

However, Perth folk are good at enjoying themselves and the millennium party on 31 December 1999 was every bit as good as the coronation and end-of-war celebrations of the past. 'What a party!' exclaimed the *Perthshire Advertiser* and proceeded to recount how 15,000 revellers on the North Inch enjoyed a 'spectacular and dazzling display of fireworks and searchlights' and how people young and old danced, sang and toasted their way into the year 2000, 'ensuring a mega-million hangover for many.' Quite a party indeed, and yet there were only four arrests for anti-social behaviour.

For all the perceived imperfections of Perth people we are a resilient bunch. We have sent our men off to all the major wars of the 20th century, leaving the women to man the home front. We have seen the decline and demise of our great home-grown industries and struggled hard to establish new ones. We have built a greater Perth, beautified the city and knocked down the slums, though in doing so we have lost some of the city's vennels, closes and quaint corners. We have released the city, to a certain extent at least, from the stranglehold of traffic. We have restored some of our great public buildings and built new ones. We have fostered the arts and encouraged sport and leisure.

Decent sanitation and public services have improved the health and eased the lives of our citizens. If that were not enough then we have also coped with changing moralities, global warming, decimalisation, emigration, immigration, pollution, drug abuse, Europe, divorce, the Internet and, for better or worse, increasing wealth. The 20th century has indeed been a century of change, and we survived it.

2010   **Stuart Cosgrove**

The People's Perth
(A publication by The Courier for Perth's 800th anniversary)

PLACES HAVE THEIR OWN unique history and identity. It really doesn't matter if it's Bath or York or Perth or Dundee, each of these places has their own narrative to tell about their life. People are fascinated by local history, that deep knowledge of an area and what its real story is, and I've certainly always found the story of Perth to be something fascinating.

Very simply, Perth is where I was born so I do have an affinity with it. It's also a place I came to in many ways, as my great-grandparents were part of the great mass migration from Ireland at the height of the famine. They came to the Perth and Dundee area at the very beginning of the jute industry – something which is a very big story in Dundee but also a story in Perth.

There was an area running through the middle of the city called the Meal Vennel, which was one of the worst and oldest Irish ghettoes in Scotland in the 1850's and 60's. It was only pulled down in my lifetime – and became effectively the St John's Centre. There was a guy called Magnus Jackson, who was one of Perth's great photographers, he mostly did botanical work and it was beautiful stuff, but because his base was around the slum dwellers, he photographed that. It's some of the best social photography seen in Britain, but largely undiscovered for that side of his work.

I stumble upon things like that and think, 'That's one of the most exciting things I've seen and it's about me, it's about my history, it's about my home town.'

I think that all people should be aware that they are temporary creations upon the earth and are part of a grand narrative. For Perth to have that grand narrative is good.

I've always considered Perth to be a city, and if anyone asks me where I come from, it's natural for me to say 'The City of Perth.' It had always been defined by the fact that the city had a cathedral – we had St Ninian's Cathedral for starters so... It has only been in the modern arena that defining what a city was became somewhat politicised and we lost out to Stirling and others. I always thought that the city where I was born deserved the city status, whatever it meant.

Of course, Perth was formerly St John's Town, and St Johnstone is the football team I support – so that's also part of that narrative.

When I was a kid in South Street, beyond where the Vennel was, there used to be an old boozer called The Olde St Johnstoun Tavern, now it's called something horrible... I don't even really want to think about it. It was one of these terrible rebranding of pubs in the Seventies that denuded them of their history. There were great bars, The Royal, The Auld Hoose, there were a few in Dundee, and still are with the likes of Mennies (The Speedwell Bar), big oak sturdy bars where there were fine wines, good beers, and they were almost like community centres. It's a great regret that The Olde St Johnstoun Tavern disappeared. It's another part of the erosion of the name... the club keeps it alive.

It keeps you ordinary, and keeps your feet on the ground. I go there with the people I grew up with, who are usually asking about my mum rather than me, which is great.

That's the thing about history – there's people's history as opposed to official history. I can look across the whole history of Perth and remember people who have simply made me smile or been part of my growing up.

For example, there was the best tablet shop in the world which belonged to a woman called Jessie McGregor. Someone would say, 'You going to Jessie McGregor's, son?' and that was something special, that wasn't just any tablet, it was Jessie McGregor's. My uncle would take me there and next door was the Black Watch headquarters, their boozer almost... A woman called Beenie Campbell, who was in her seventies if not older, would be marching up and down outside, swearing and shouting at the top of her voice 'Black Watch yi *** yi'll nivver ***** die!'

Living in the media, it's important to know that you belong somewhere. You can be stripped of a real identity in the media so that's why Perth is important to me.

2010   **Peter Ross**

Fair Play to Perth (from *Scotland on Sunday*)

As the town – or is it a city? - celebrates its 800th anniversary, its inhabitants reveal what makes the place tick, and why they hate Dundee so much.

In his grand office with its view of the Tay, Provost John Hulbert is sitting beneath a stern 19th-century oil painting of one of his predecessors and explaining why Perth, the town over which he presides, ought to be made a city. 'It's a matter of dignity and prestige,' he says. 'Perth lost its city status in 1975, which I think was quite unjust.'

This was the local government re-organisation of that year, when regions and districts replaced the historic shires. Since then, Perth has had to content itself with being a town, but it has never quite reconciled itself to the relegation. Now, with local football club St Johnstone back in the SPL, the dignitaries of Perth fancy their chances of a similar promotion. So in this, the 800th anniversary of Perth being confirmed as a royal burgh, the local council is lobbying Westminster to make it a city once more.

The people of Perth, meanwhile, believe quite simply that they live in a city and are surprised when I mention that, actually, they don't. 'Yer kiddin'!' says a sallow man smoking outside the Robert Burns Lounge. 'Wait till ah tell them inside.'

Such confusion is understandable. Road signs welcome visitors, pointedly, to the City of Perth, and everyone here knows it as The Fair City – a title bestowed by Sir Walter Scott. He set his novel *'The Fair Maid of Perth'* here, and considered the county the most beautiful in Scotland.

On a cold, drizzly January day, however, Perth does not look its best. Gritty brown ice is heaped in every gutter like a range of manky glaciers.

However, there is still a sense of how pretty it can be. Cloud shrouds the tops of the hills that run down to the north bank of the Tay, their slopes dusted with snow and dotted with the stone villas of the wealthy. Broad churches and narrow vennels mean that Perth itself has retained much of its historic character.

As a fine Scottish town, Perth is convincing. As a city, less so. With a population of around 45,000, it just doesn't have the scale. It doesn't feel like Glasgow or Edinburgh. There's none of that sense of possibility and low-level threat. Also, cities are conceptual – when we say their name, we understand what they are all about. Perth, by contrast, is a cypher. There's no real prevailing idea. It seems important, though, to try to understand Perth, its traits and values, and for this it is necessary to meet the people.

My first stop is Wilkie's Music House. In a room lined with musical instruments, the shop owner Bill Wilkie pulls together two piano stools so we can talk. Wilkie is 88, Perth born and bred, and has run this shop for half a century. He is well-known locally as the impresario behind the All Scotland Accordion and Fiddle Championships which he has staged in the town since 1949. 'I'm dodderin' a bit now,' he says, 'but we manage.' His grandson, Richard Colburn, drums with Snow Patrol and Belle And Sebastian.

Wilkie is dressed neatly in blazer, beige cardie and tie, and answers to Totty Wee. This nickname, given to him by his late friend Peter Sellers, is a reference to both his size and his enjoyment, on occasion, of a small whisky. He and Sellers toured India together between 1944 and 1945 as part of the RAF Gang Shows. Sellers played the drums and did comic routines; Totty Wee played the accordion and tried not to let the dengue fever put him off his stroke.

When Wilkie talks about what makes Perth special, he could be talking about himself. 'It's a friendly place for a start,' he says, 'and not too big.' He's old enough to remember when cattle grazed on Perth's parks – 'You had to watch where you put your feet' – and feels it has suited him to live here. He enjoys being part of the public life. That's why he continues to work way past the age of retirement and to stage his concerts – he likes the people. It's a respectful, conservative place, he says, but there's a hint of cheek as well. He and his dance band have performed over the years at most of the party conferences held at Perth City Hall. He has met and played for many prime ministers including Heath, Wilson and Douglas-Home. 'Maggie Thatcher was doing her walk around and we were playing "Over The Rainbow," he recalls, "She comes up and says, Over The Rainbow? My favourite is, Who's Taking You Home Tonight? And I remember thinking, "It'll likely be that big detective standing behind you."'

A few minutes walk away, on the High Street, it's a quiet moment in Afishyonados, a chip shop which suggests that in Perth even the punning names of fast food places are a cut above. 'Well, it's always been the Fair City, hasn't it?' says the man behind the counter in the baseball cap, when I ask about the issue of city status.

'I was the Fair Maid once,' says his colleague, a middle-aged woman with bobbed hair leaning through the hatch leading to the adjoining cafe. 'It was for the Perthshire Advertiser in 1971.' The paper published a photograph of a different 'Fair Maid' – an attractive local girl – every month. 'I had my photo taken on the bonnet of a car,' the woman recalls, dreamily. 'It was a Vauxhall.'

'I really think that to be a city you need to have a university,' says the man in the cap. 'Or at least a John Lewis.'

Across the street is the sort of shop I expected to see in Perth. P.D. Malloch has been selling fishing tackle and the like since the 19th century. It's a beautiful place, wood–panelled, with rows of guns and rods for sale. Drawers slide out of an old cabinet to reveal hundreds of fishing flies, including my namesake, the Peter Ross, which is deadly for sea trout. Mounted on one wall is the head of a great horned kudo, shot by John Buntin, the shop's owner. 'He actually got it crossing the Tay one morning,' jokes Hugh Mailer, who works here, and who ties flies known as Shug's Bugs.

'We do look at ourselves as country folk,' says Buntin when I ask whether Perth still retains its rural character. 'A lot of people still fish and shoot.' So does that mean Perth is posh? 'We had a countess in two days ago and you wouldn't have called her posh,' says John's wife Elaine. 'No–one can be posh,' says Mailer, 'when they're trying on a pair of wellies.'

Perth's hoity–toity reputation is a bugbear of the broadcaster Stuart Cosgrove, who grew up in Letham, one of the housing schemes which skirt the centre. 'They are as socially deprived as any in the west of Scotland,' he says. 'But there's this curious thing where, in order to portray Perth as the Range Rover capital of Scotland, half of the citizens have been airbrushed out of the story. There's a fake stereotype that Glasgow is working class and has authenticity and places like Perth are somehow fake. It's a weird thing that has been allowed to fester as a belief.'

If it is sometimes hard to define Perth, it is easy to say what it is not: Dundee. The rivalry between the two is intense, particularly when it comes to the football. When St Johnstone play Dundee, the crowd at McDiarmid Park doubles in size.

On Friday afternoon, Bruce McAlpine, an eagle-featured man who has worked on the door for St Johnstone since 1976, is considering fetching his shovel to clear ice from the pitch. ' "We hate Dundee and we hate Dundee", that's what we sing. There's nae chorus,' he explains.

And does the emnity on the pitch mirror a larger rivalry between the two places? 'I'm sure it does. We've got far better scenery for one thing. The Tay starts here. They just get it when we're finished with it.' One of my colleagues is a Dundonian, I tell McAlpine, who feels that people from Perth look down on them. He nods eagerly, 'We do.'

In the Royal Bar, a busy and old-fashioned pub, Jamie Beatson is unwinding after work. He's 23 and runs the We Are Perth website which covers football and local culture. He works in Dundee, but it would be against his very nature to move there. 'I love Perth, which is unusual. People my age tend to move off to uni and not come back. I sometimes wonder if the young, educated heart is being ripped out of Perth. But for me, walking down to the River Tay is just beautiful.'

I take Beatson's advice and end my day in Perth with a stroll by the river. It's the first day of the salmon season, but too cold for fishing. I am not alone, however, in admiring the view.

'1766 that was built,' says Gordon Muir, a retired police officer in a long black coat, gesturing towards the graceful arches of a bridge. Though originally a Fifer, Muir joined what was then Perth City Police in 1956, and his love for the place is deep. He has, in fact, been moved to write a song and is not shy of singing it.

'Be it summertime or winter,' he croons, visibly moved. 'You'd be best to make your way/To that fairest of all cities on the green banks of the Tay.'

* * *

2011 **George MacDiarmid**

Perth My Fair City

The summer days dawning with floral perfume,
Romancing by Rodney by the bright shining moon;
Young children play on the Inches for fun
In Perth's fair city where my life first began.

The silvery Tay serenades our night's sleep
And passes St Matthew's where Christian folks meet;
I've wandered the world but no place can compare
With Perth's fair city and the friends I've made there.

To the braes of old Craigie in deep winter snow
Like fine alpine slopes, the sledgers would go.
St Leonard's in springtime in sunshine does glow,
And in Perth's fair city golden daffodils grow.

At the Kirk of St John's where pilgrims still call
There's peace there a plenty for one and for all;
And if God should ordain it, I'll take a Perth bride
And, like the Black Watch, in that fair city reside.

So join in this song and sing with me now
Of grey cobbled streets and the silver spruce bow.
The hill of Kinnoull in mists I recall
And dancing with fair maids in Perth's city hall.

* * *

Kenneth Roy

'They've just given city status to the wrong town.'
(from the Scottish Review of March 15, 2012)

EARLIER THIS YEAR on a visit to Perth, whose restoration of city status was announced yesterday, I was checked into the
Salutation Hotel by a man who knew too much about my past.

'You'll remember the cheery barmaid,' he said – cheerily enough.

'The cheery barmaid,' I repeated dumbly.

'Yes, the one you met here,' he continued in the same discon-
certing fashion.

Perth – the Salutation Hotel – a barmaid – my mind was racing.

'The Rotary Club was meeting that day,' he added helpfully.

'Oh, that day,' I lied.

'Well,' he said, 'she doesn't work here any more.'

'She doesn't?'

'No, we don't have any cheery barmaids in the hotel now.'

'Why not?'

'Because,' he replied, 'we've got cheery barmen instead.'

Feeling slightly dazed, I picked up the room key and
wandered through to the bar. It occurred to me that Charles Edward
Stuart stayed in this hotel, in the olden days when the Salutation ran
to cheery barmaids. Perhaps that hopeless character had been
distracted by one of them. It might explain a lot.

Sure enough it was a man who was serving the drinks. Only
he wasn't cheery, not a bit. He had the look of a fellow who had
just received some extremely bad news – the Rangers result, maybe.
I ordered myself a glass of dry white wine, the first of several that
evening, to fortify myself for the ordeal.

Oh, I've missed a bit. Before I left reception, the other man –
the manager type – had solved the mystery of the cheery barmaid.

In 1987 – yes, they have long memories in Perth – there are people still alive in the town – sorry, city – who remember giving bonnie Prince Charlie an encouraging wave as he arrived at the Salutation off his sturdy mare – it seems that in 1987 I did a chapter on Perth for a book of miscellaneous travels.

Here is the passage in question:

I gave my lunchtime custom to the Salutation, which advertises itself as the oldest established hotel in Scotland (1699). Upstairs, the Rotary Club of Perth was preparing to meet in a room next to the bar. An official sat at a table just inside the door, ticking off names of Members Attending.

I asked the barmaid (25 years later she would be immortalised as the cheery barmaid) for directions to St John's Church.

'St John's Kirk,' she corrected me, 'We aye call it Kirk.'

'Kirk it is, then.'

'My daughter's gettin' married there next year. For weddings, you pay somebody a fiver and they'll ring the bells. Lovely when they ring the bells.'

'I'm sure…'

She laughed. 'Easy pleased, I am!'

I explained that I was going to St John's Kirk for the opening event of the Perth Festival. The barmaid said that the festival was great, and getting better every year. But when I remarked on the flags (there were a lot of flags hanging around that day) she said that she doubted if they were connected with the festival. More likely, she thought, the flags were for the opening of the new shopping centre.

Personally, she didn't want the new shopping centre. It would only take trade away from the High Street. Already, two chainstores had decided to quit and relocate in the St John's Centre. What would happen to their old premises? What would happen to the High Street generally?

So she really was the cheery barmaid. She will be quite an old woman now, if she's still alive, and her daughter, for whom the bells tolled for a fiver, will be celebrating her silver wedding next year, if she's still married. But, as well as being famously cheery, she was also a prophet in her own land. She saw, as few did, the folly of these new shopping centres and was among the first to predict the inevitable result, the decline of our traditional High Streets. Look at them now.

After the speech* – that was the particular ordeal in January 2012 to which I alluded earlier – a woman came up to me with a rebuke.

'I do hope Scotland isn't as depressing as you made it out to be tonight,' she said.

I had not spoken of Perth, although I might easily have done. There is a subterranean problem of homelessness in the city and district which ought to temper any mood of complacent self-congratulation.

Some years ago at the Young Scotland Programme, there was a tense exchange after dinner when two of the delegates, both homeless young people living in Perth, sometimes on the streets, sometimes in hostels, challenged a local politician who happened to be with us as a speaker. They wanted to know what was being done about homelessness in Perth, and were shocked and angry when the politician denied its existence. Their distress was palpable.

The situation of these young people did not improve. One of them – a girl of nineteen in poor physical health – died not long afterwards. I lost touch with the other delegate, a bright articulate man, I wish I knew what happened to him.

'I do hope Scotland isn't as depressing as you made it out to be tonight.'

Get real, woman. But there is a keener sense of reality in some towns than in others – a greater awareness of the poverty and disadvantage lurking not far from Debenham's front door.

If we must have royal celebrations, and if we must have new cities to mark them, I would have given the honour in Scotland to a town less pleased with itself.

Kenneth Roy was the principal speaker at the 2012 Annual Dinner of the Perth Burns Club.

2012   Her Majesty the Queen

The Queen's speech in Perth on 6 July 2012
on the occasion of the granting of city status

PROVOST,

PRINCE PHILIP AND I are very pleased to be with you today and to be back in Scotland during our Jubilee tour of the United Kingdom. Scotland has played such a very special part in our lives, and that of my family, over the years and we have greatly enjoyed our frequent visits.

Scotland's extraordinary contribution to the history of the nation over the centuries is well documented and the City of Perth, which sits at the very heart of Scotland, has through hundreds of years played such an important part in this remarkable story. Perth was, of course, the ancient Capital of Scotland, the crowning place of Scottish Kings and only recently celebrated 800 years of its own history.

I have many happy memories of previous visits to Perth, including the opening of the Queens Bridge in 1960 and more recently the opening of Perth Concert Hall.

Today, we have great pleasure in visiting the City of Perth at the end of our Scottish Tour. I would like to congratulate you all warmly on the restoration of City Status. It is an accolade that is well earned and Prince Philip and I extend to all of you, to your families both in Perth and the surrounding area of Perthshire and Kinross, our very best wishes for the future and our thanks for welcoming us here so generously today.

* * *

Biographies & Bibliography

HENRY ADAMSON (*bap.*1581, *d.*1637)
Classical poet, historian, and schoolmaster, born in Perth. He wrote *Muses Threnodie*, a poetical effusion on the history of Perth and its antiquities, which is an important account of life in seventeenth-century Perth.
His father, James Adamson, a Provost of Perth, was Dean of Guild in 1600, the year of the Gowrie Conspiracy.

PETER AGNEW (1793–?)
Talented violinist and landscape artist. Born in Perth's South Street, he moved to Glasgow as a youth and worked as a house painter. He spent several years in London, supporting himself as a musician and artist, before returning to Glasgow.

DAVID (D.) BROWN ANDERSON (*fl.*1901)
Writer from the Isle of Wight.

IAIN BANKS (1954–2013)
Leading literary novelist from Fife, who also wrote science fiction under the name Iain M. Banks. In 2008, *The Times* named him in their list of 'The 50 Greatest British Writers Since 1945'.

PETER BAXTER (1860–1936)
One of Perth's greatest historians, and a Bailie on Perth Town Council. He wrote the two-volume *Perth: Past and Present*, *The Drama in Perth*, *Football in Perthshire*, *Golf in Perth and Perthshire*, *The Shoemaker Incorporation of Perth* and many other books on Perth's history.

ARTHUR KINMOND (A. K.) BELL (1868-1942)
Philanthropist and son of the founder of the whisky dynasty of Arthur Bell & Sons Ltd. He turned the company into a multinational organisation. His Gannochy Trust has given many benefits to the city he loved.

JOHN JOY (J. J.) BELL (1871-1934)
Glasgow journalist and author whose many articles described the lives of working-class Glaswegians. He is best known for creating the character Wee MacGreegor for his *Glasgow Evening Times* articles, later published in book form.

REVEREND ANDREW KENNEDY HUTCHISON (K.H.) BOYD (1825-1899)

Moderator of the General Assembly of the Church of Scotland who preached latterly at St Andrews. He wrote for several magazines during the mid to late 1800s.

LYSBETH BRAZIER (1918-1964)

Perth-born songwriter who penned the lyrics of *The Hill of Kinnoull* for the Scottish singing duo The Alexander Brothers. The music was composed by *Perthshire Advertiser* photographer Harry Robertson and the song was first performed in Perth Theatre's 1963 Summer Show season.

GEOFF BROWN

Founder of a prominent Perthshire building company and, from 1986 to 2011, chairman of St Johnstone Football Club, a role now held by his son Steve. He instigated the club's move from their ailing 1920s ground to a new custom-built stadium.

JOHN BUCHAN, first BARON TWEEDSMUIR (1875-1940)

Scottish novelist, historian, and Unionist politician, born in York Place, Perth. In 1935 he became the fifteenth governor-general of Canada, a position he held until his death. His many adventure fiction novels include *The Thirty-Nine Steps*, *Greenmantle* and *Prester John*.

FRANCIS BUCHANAN (1825–*c*.1895)

Perth draper who later moved to Sheffield but never lost his love for his home town. His poems and songs show how deeply the scenes of his early years were engraved in his memory.

ROBERT BURNS (1759–1796)

Scotland's national bard visited Perth once, on 14 September, 1787, lodging overnight at Croom's Tavern in the High Street. He and his travelling companion William Nicol were nearing the end of a three-week tour of the Highlands collecting Scotland's almost-forgotten traditional music.

ALEXANDER CAMPBELL (1764-1824)

Scottish musician, composer, and miscellaneous writer. In his later years he fell into great poverty and made his living by copying manuscripts for Sir Walter Scott, one of his former pupils.

SIR JOHN CARR (1722-1807)

County Durham-born schoolmaster and writer. He is best known for his five-volume *Translation of Lucian* from ancient Greek, which took him almost twenty-five years.

ROBERT CHAMBERS (1802-1871)
Prolific writer, most famous for his enjoyable reference books. Along with his older brother, William, he began in business as a bookseller in Edinburgh and wrote in his spare time. In 1832, the brothers formed the Edinburgh publishing house of W. & R.Chambers which was to have great influence on both sides of the Atlantic. His later years were spent in St Andrews.

WILLIAM CLYDE (1791-1873)
A lyric poet of considerable culture. The son of a Perth bookseller, he moved to London in 1825. His later years were spent in what has been described as 'semi-genteel poverty' in Perth.

LORD HENRY THOMAS COCKBURN (1779-1854)
Scottish lawyer, judge, and literary figure. He served as Solicitor General for Scotland between 1830 and 1834.

BILLY CONNOLLY
Scottish comedian, musician, presenter, and actor. Originally a Glasgow shipyard worker, in recent years he has featured in a number of films and television travel programmes.

STUART COSGROVE
Journalist, broadcaster, and television executive, born and educated in Perth. He is currently director of creative diversity at Channel 4 Television and co-presenter of a weekly football programme on BBC Radio Scotland. He was awarded an honorary Doctorate of Arts by the University of Abertay, Dundee, and honorary professorships by the University of Stirling and Liverpool John Moores University.

ASHLEY REGINALD COURTENAY (*fl.*1956)
Travel writer famed for his guides to over seven hundred hotels and inns throughout Britain. All were personally visited and recommended by Mr and Mrs Courtenay.

BRIAN COX
Dundee-born actor internationally known for his appearances in many Hollywood productions including *Rushmore*, *X-Men United* and *Troy*. He is also known for his work with the Royal Shakespeare Company.

DANIEL DEFOE (*c.*1660-1731)
English trader, writer, journalist, and pamphleteer, credited as being one of the founders of the English novel. Best known for his first novel, *Robinson Crusoe*, he wrote over five hundred publications on various topics including politics, crime, religion and the supernatural.

DR THOMAS FROGNALL DIBDIN (1776-1847)
British bibliographer, and clergyman born in Calcutta, India.

JOHN DICKSON (1817-1909)
A member of the Society of Writers to the *Signet*. Originally from Kirkcud-brightshire, he had a long and active career in Perth's legal profession.

ELIZABETH DIGGLE (*fl.*1788)
English writer from Kent. In 1788 she published a journal of thirty-two let-ters sent to her sister and other relatives during an exhausting four-month tour of England and Scotland in her own carriage, accompanied by her aunt and a servant.

JEREMY DUNCAN
Perth author with a longstanding interest in the city's history. For many years he was the local studies librarian for Perth & Kinross Libraries.

DOUGLAS EADIE
Scottish writer, film director, and television producer. He was born in Perth, educated at Perth Academy and now lives in Fife.

SIR NICHOLAS HARDWICK FAIRBAIRN (1933-1995)
Scottish advocate and politician, elected as MP for Kinross & West Perthshire in 1974 and 1979 and for Perth & Kinross in 1983, 1987 and 1992. He served as Solicitor General for Scotland from 1979 to 1982 and was known for his outspoken manner and flamboyant dress style.

BARTHÉLEMY FAUJAS DE SAINT-FOND (1741-1819)
French geologist, traveller, and commissioner for mines. He travelled to most European countries, where he observed rock formations and the natural environment. He was the first to recognise the volcanic nature of the columns of Fingal's Cave in Staffa.

MALCOLM FERGUSON (*c.*1823-1900)
A keen angler and mountain climber who wrote several books on rambling and touring in Scotland. Born at Morenish near Killin, he moved to Glasgow in his youth and found work as a storekeeper before founding the firm of Malcolm Ferguson & Company. He is credited with erecting the cairn on Ben Lawers.

THE REVEREND SAMUEL FERGUSON (1828-1869)
Perth clergyman and author of a poem in praise of Queen Victoria's first visit to Scotland. This work, in six cantos, with notes, runs to 214 octavo

pages. On the day of its publication, 27 September 1869, the author, mistaking his way, walked into the River Tay at Perth and was drowned.

DR WILLIAM H. FINDLAY (1912-2006)

One of the founders of the Perth Civic Trust and an associate of the Royal Photographic Society. Most of his working life was spent in the hospital service in Perth, but his main leisure interest was photography.

(WILLIAM) IAN ROBERTSON FINLAY (1906-1995)

Writer, broadcaster, art historian, and director of the Royal Scottish Museum, Edinburgh. He originated or promoted many major exhibitions for the Edinburgh International Festival and was a Freeman of the City of London.

DUNCAN FRASER (1905-1977)

Glasgow-born schoolteacher, and journalist. On a visit to Montrose, he met his future wife Dora, whose family owned Standard Press printers and publishers. After some time in Glasgow, he accepted the invitation to join the family business and he was appointed editor of the *Montrose Standard* newspaper. He wrote sixteen books on east and central Scotland, including *Highland Perthshire* and the annually published *Discovering East Scotland*.

JOHN GEDDIE (1846-1927)

Journalist, editor, biographer, Fellow of the Royal Geographical Society, and author of several books. He wrote the introduction to *Illustrations of the Scenery of the River Tay* for the Royal Association for the Promotion of the Fine Arts in Scotland. This book, with its watercolour drawings by Sir William Fettes Douglas, R. B. Nisbet, Charles H. Mackie and James Paterson, was reproduced in photogravure by T. & R. Annan, Glasgow.

COLIN GIBSON (1907-1998)

Artist, author and journalist best known for his 'Nature Diary' column which appeared in *The Courier* each Saturday for over fifty years.

ANN GLOAG

Perth-born co-founder of the Stagecoach bus group, with her brother Brian Souter. She is now a non-executive director of the business and devotes much of her time to charity causes.

SETON PAUL GORDON (1886-1977)

Scottish naturalist, photographer, folklorist, and writer of many books describing the wildlife and scenery of Scotland. He was awarded the CBE in 1939 for his services to natural history.

DAVID GRAHAM-CAMPBELL (1913-1994)
Head of history at Eton and Warden of Trinity College, Glenalmond.
He was originally from London but lived latterly in Perth.

ELIZABETH GRANT OF ROTHIEMURCHUS (1797-1885)
Edinburgh society figure and land improver. Born in Edinburgh's New
Town, she spent most of her childhood in London and on the family estate
at Rothiemurchus on Speyside. In 1827 her family left Scotland for India
where she met and married Colonel Henry Smith. Her later life was spent
managing and improving her husband's inherited but impoverished estate
at Baltyboys near Dublin.

THE REVEREND SAMUEL GOSNELL GREEN (1822-1905)
Baptist pastor, scholar, editor, and children's educator who made many
visits to Scotland. His descriptions and opinions provided the Victorian
tourist with a perceptive guide to the country.

THE REVEREND H. ARMSTRONG HALL (*fl.*1892)
Minister of St John the Baptist Episcopal Church, Perth, from 1892 to 1898.

THE REVEREND JAMES HALL (*fl.*1803)
Traveller and chaplain to the Earl of Caithness. Born in Clackmannan and
educated at the University of St Andrews, he later moved to Walthamstow,
Essex. During his 1803 tour of Scotland, he kept mainly to the coastline
but followed the banks of the River Tay, taking in Perth.

DR ALBERT W. (BILL) HARDING (1929-2011)
Teacher, lecturer, researcher, and author. Born in Angus and brought up in
Perth, he was a graduate of the Universities of London, St Andrews,
Dundee, Glasgow and Strathclyde, and a Fellow of the Educational Institute
of Scotland. He also won a Page Scholarship to the United States.

ROBERT HERON (1764-1807)
Scottish writer, teacher, and French translator. He lived beyond his means
and eventually died in a debtors' prison in London.

ROWLAND HILL (1744-1833)
Popular English evangelical preacher, and influential advocate of smallpox
vaccination. He was founder and resident of the independent Surrey
Chapel, London. Rowland Hill, the instigator of penny postage, is believed
to have been named after him.

EDWIN PAXTON HOOD (1820-1885)
Nonconformist and writer. Born in London, the son of a seaman, he edited the *Eclectic and Congregational Review* for some years and had many books published.

JOHN (JACK) HOUSE (1906-1991)
Popular writer and broadcaster from Tollcross (now in Glasgow).

QUINTIN JARDINE
Scottish crime writer, well-known for his popular Bob Skinner and Oz Blackstone novels.

ROY KERRIDGE
London-based freelance writer and journalist who has travelled extensively throughout the UK, Ireland and the American Deep South. He has written several books on his adventures.

MAGGIE LENNON
Founder of The Bridges Programmes charity and fellowship director of the Institute of Contemporary Scotland. Born in Dundee, she is a former editor of the *Weekend Scotsman*.

JOHN LETTICE (1737-1832)
English clergyman, translator, academic, and writer who tutored many English notables. He was chaplain to the ninth Duke of Hamilton from 1804 until 1832.

DR JOHN LEYDEN (1775-1811)
Scottish Orientalist who assisted Sir Walter Scott in collecting materials for his *Minstrelsy of the Scottish Border*. Scott wrote of him 'Dr John Leyden, a name which will not soon be forgotten in Scottish literature'. Born near Hawick, he spent his later years in India, first on the medical staff of the general hospital in Madras, and latterly in Calcutta as a professor of Hindustani and a commissioner in the court of requests. He died of malaria during an expedition to Java.

R. F. MACKENZIE (1910-1987)
Adventurer, journalist, and teacher born the son of an Aberdeenshire stationmaster. He cycled around Europe in the 1930s. Following war service with Bomber Command, Mackenzie taught in Galashiels, Fife and finally in Aberdeen. He was a strong campaigner for a more progressive eduction system and the abolition of corporal punishment in schools.

JOHN MACKY (*d.*1726)

Scottish spy, the first person to inform the British of James II's intended invasion of England in 1692. His network of spies was crucial to the discovery, in 1708, of Jacobite plans to invade Scotland.

GEORGE MacDIARMID

Entertainer and songwriter. A native of Mull, he has lived in Perth for over forty years.

MAGNUS MAGNUSSON (1929-2007)

Journalist, translator, writer, and television presenter. He was born in Iceland but lived most of his life in Scotland, and was best known for hosting the BBC television programme *Mastermind* for twenty-five years.

PETER MARTIN

Author of the acclaimed *Life of James Boswell*, and a professor of English who has taught in England and the United States. He has also written books on English literature and garden history.

DAVID McCORMACK (1886-1964)

Perth writer, poet, and theatre critic whose later years were spent in Glasgow.

PROVOST JEAN McCORMACK

Perthshire businesswoman and Provost of Perth & Kinross between 1991 and 1996.

DAVID W. McFADDEN

Canadian writer who has published over twenty books of poetry and prose. He lives in Toronto.

WILLIAM TOPAZ McGONAGALL (*c.*1825-1902)

Scottish weaver, doggerel poet, and actor who has been called the worst poet in British history. His work forms part of a long tradition of verses about events and tragedies which were widely distributed as handbills.

MORAY McLAREN (1901-1971)

Author, critic, playwright, and broadcaster. He was assistant editor of *The London Mercury* before joining the BBC, where he became the first assistant editor of *The Listener* and later Scotland's first programme director. In the Second World War he was attached to the Foreign Office and appointed head of the Polish Region Political Intelligence Department. He journeyed round Scotland on horseback to gain colour for a novel on James Boswell and Samuel Johnson's Highland and Hebridean tour.

ALEXANDER McLEISH (*c*.1850-1933)
Poet and songwriter. Believed to be a Perth plumber who wrote about his home town in his spare time.

LAWRENCE MELVILLE (1871-1941)
Lawyer, farmer, and writer. Author of *The Fair Land of Gowrie* and *Errol: it's legends, lands and people*. He lived at Northbank, Errol, Perthshire.

HAMISH MILES (1894-1937)
Writer, literary adviser, and translator.

ASCOTT ROBERT (A. R.) HOPE MONCRIEFF (1846-1927)
Author, editor, and translator. He wrote around two hundred books, many of historical and topographical interest. He also wrote novels, school books, picture books, travel guides and, under the pseudonym Ascott R. Hope, books for boys.

THE REVEREND THOMAS MORER (1651-1715)
Minister of St Ann's-within-Aldersgate who became chaplain to a Scottish regiment.

HENRY VOLLAM (H. V.) MORTON (1892-1979)
Journalist and pioneering travel writer best known for his popular books on Britain and the Holy Land. Born in Lancashire, in 1913 he moved to London where he worked on the *Daily Mail*, *Evening Standard* and *Daily Express*.

DR JAMES MORTON (1922-1986)
Assistant professor and director of the Lung Function Laboratory in the University of British Columbia medical faculty in Vancouver. Of Perth ancestry, he was the writer of several books on British Columbia.

SARAH MURRAY (née MAESE) (1744-1811)
English travel writer who published under the name The Hon. Mrs Murray of Kensington. Her first husband was the Hon. William Murray, brother of the Earl of Dunmore. After his death she married George Aust, a retired Permanent Under-Secretary of State at the Foreign Office.

CAMPBELL NAIRNE
Scottish novelist with strong Perth connections. Author of *Stony Ground*, and the classic *One Stair Up*, about an Edinburgh working class family.

WILLIAM THOMAS NEWTE (1746-1817)

Pseudonymous author of memoirs, biographies, travel books, and Scripture commentaries. His real name was William Thomson. Born in the Perthshire parish of Forteviot, he was librarian to Thomas Hay, eighth Earl of Kinnoull, at Dupplin Castle, before becoming a parish minister. He later settled in London, where he embarked on his thirty-five year writing career.

GRAHAM OGILVY

Dundee-based author, journalist, and correspondent for several leading newspapers and magazines.

THE REVEREND DAVID D. OGSTON (1945-2008)

Writer, known for his poems and work in the Scots language (particularly the Doric). A native of Aberdeenshire, he was minister of St John's Kirk in Perth from 1980 until shortly before his death in 2008. His name appeared regularly in Scottish publications.

CAROLINA OLIPHANT, BARONESS NAIRNE (1766-1845)

One of Scotland's most famous songwriters. Born in 'the auld hoose of Gask', Perthshire, to a prominent Jacobite family, she married her second cousin William M. Nairne, who became Baron Nairne in 1824. Like Robert Burns, she was a collector of Scotland's national airs. About eighty-seven songs (originals and cobblings) carry her signature, though during her lifetime they appeared under the pseudonym Mrs Bogan of Bogan. Her range is very wide, with the sentimental and sincere Jacobite ones among her best liked.

LUCY PARKER (*fl.*1863)

Diarist from Barnet, Hertfordshire, who recorded her family's travels.

THOMAS PENNANT (1726-1798)

Welsh naturalist and antiquary known for his writings on natural history, geology and geographical expeditions. *A Tour in Scotland*, published in 1769, proved so popular that it was followed by the publication of a second Scottish journey in 1774. These works have proved invaluable in preserving the record of antiquarian relics.

GEORGE PENNY (1771-1850)

Perth historian best known for his *Traditions of Perth* (1836), a fascinating account of the town from 1770 to 1830. He was first a weaver, then a journalist, and became the publisher of the *Perthshire Advertiser* and *Strathmore Journal*.

WILLIAM STRATFORD (W. S.) PERCY (1872-1946)

Australian actor and travel writer who moved to London in 1913.

BISHOP RICHARD POCOCKE (1704-1765)

Writer, diarist and traveller. Born in Southampton in 1704, he became Bishop of Ossory and Meath in Ireland. From 1737 to 1742 he visited Egypt, Palestine, Mesopotamia, Syria and Cyprus and published two volumes under the title, *A Description of the East and of some other Countries*. His tour of Scotland lasted five months and covered most parts of the country.

BEATRIX POTTER (1866-1943)

Author and illustrator. The daughter of a wealthy London family, she developed her interest in wildlife, drawing and painting during childhood summers spent at Dalguise House and other large properties in the Dunkeld area. Her diaries reveal her as a lonely child engaged in solitary pursuits. It was in Perthshire that she gained the inspiration for creating Peter Rabbit and her other famous animal characters.

DR ROBERT RITCHIE (1903-1990)

Perth general practitioner and Lord Provost of Perth from 1963 to 1966.

PETER ROSS

Journalist, broadcaster, and regular feature writer for *The Scotsman*. He is the author of the recently published book *Daunderlust: Dispatches from Unreported Scotland*, a selection of his articles from *Scotland on Sunday*.

WILLIAM ROUGHEAD (1870-1952)

Edinburgh lawyer and prolific 1930s writer with an interest in modern and historical Scottish crime, and particularly Scottish murder trials.

KENNETH ROY

Journalist, author and former BBC news and current affairs anchorman. He founded West Sound Radio in 1981, the magazine *Scottish Review* in 1995, the Institute of Contemporary Scotland in 2000, and the Young Scotland Programme in 2002. He has published six books.

JOHN RUSKIN (1819-1900)

Writer, draughtsman, watercolourist, social thinker, philanthropist, and the leading English art critic of the Victorian era. He wrote on subjects ranging from geology to architecture, myth to ornithology, literature to education, and history to political economy. Two of his childhood years were spent in Perth. In 1848 he married Effie Gray of Bowerswell, the daughter of family friends. The marriage was annulled in 1854 and Effie married the artist John Everett Millais the following year.

MICHAEL W. RUSSELL MSP
Scottish Education Secretary and former journalist, television producer, and director. In 1998 he retraced portions of Edwin Muir's famous journey from the Lowlands to the Highlands in Depression-era Scotland, to discover how much the country and its people have changed over the decades.

SIR WALTER SCOTT (1771-1832)
Historical novelist, playwright, and poet. He was the first Scottish author to have a truly international career during his lifetime, with contemporary readers in Europe, Australia and North America. Many of his works remain classics of both English-language and Scottish literature. Scott had strong connections with the Perth area. In his early twenties he had a romantic association with Wilhelmina Belches who was related to the Belches of Invermay near Forteviot and he regularly visited her there. His aunt, Miss Christian Rutherford, lived at Pitcullen. Scott was a member of the Literary and Antiquarian Society of Perth, and his famous novel *The Fair Maid of Perth* is set in the town.

WILLIAM SOUTAR (1898-1943)
Poet and diarist. During his lifetime he published nine volumes of verse, another was printed privately, and two were published posthumously. He died at the age of forty-five, after a crippling illness which had seen him confined to bed at his parents' home in Wilson Street, Perth, for thirteen years.

CAMPBELL STEVEN (1911-2002)
Scottish writer with a particular interest in mountaineering, island-going and bird-watching. He lived latterly in Aberfeldy and regularly contributed articles to *Scottish Field* and other magazines.

JOHN TAYLOR (1578-1653)
Ferry-boy, naval man, waterman, and traveller-poet. Born in Gloucester and known as 'the Water Poet,' he made a number of journeys through parts of England, Scotland and the Continent. During a three-month journey from London to Scotland and back in 1618, he travelled mainly on foot.

ARTHUR ALEXANDER (A. A.) THOMSON (1894-1968)
Civil servant and author best known for his books on cricket. He wrote nearly sixty books, including plays, novels, verse, humour and travel books. He was a drama critic and columnist for the *Radio Times*. In 1968 he was awarded the MBE for services to sports writing.

NIGEL TRANTER (1909-2000)
Scottish historian and author, famous for his historical fiction and non-fiction novels, Scottish travel books, children's books and westerns. He was awarded the OBE in 1983 for his services to literature.

THOMAS TUCKER (*fl.*1655)
Register to the Commission for the Excise in England. He was sent to Scotland 'to give his assistance in settling the excise and custom there'. When he visited Perth in 1655, Scotland was occupied by an English army under Oliver Cromwell.

VICTORIA, QUEEN OF GREAT BRITAIN (1819-1901)
A diarist from the age of thirteen (when she was Princess Victoria of Kent) until shortly before her death. The diaries of her visits to Scotland have been described as among the happiest books ever written, reflecting her appreciation of the dramatic Highland scenery and her love for the Scottish people.

IAN WALLACE (1919-2009)
English bass-baritone opera and concert singer, actor and broadcaster, of Scottish extraction.

JACK WEBSTER
Journalist and author of seventeen books. Born in Maud, Aberdeenshire, he worked for the *Turriff Advertiser* and *The Press and Journal* and *Evening Express* before becoming one of Scotland's leading feature writers with the *Scottish Daily Express*. Later, he was a popular columnist with *The Herald*. In 2000 he was awarded an honorary degree from the University of Aberdeen.

TOM WEIR (1914-2006)
Scottish mountaineer, author, photographer, and broadcaster, best known for his long-running television series *Weir's Way* and his monthly articles which appeared in *The Scots Magazine* for over fifty years. He was awarded the MBE in 1978.

MAJOR-GENERAL JAMES PETER WOLFE (1727-1759)
British army officer famed for his victory over the French at the 1759 Battle of Quebec, where he died from injuries sustained during the battle. He was an officer at the battles of Falkirk and Culloden during the Jacobite uprising of 1745-6. From 1748 to 1756 he was on garrison duty in Scotland.

* * *

SELECTED BIBLIOGRAPHY

BOOKS

Aitken, William Russell (editor), P*oems of William Soutar: A New Selection* (Edinburgh: Scottish Academic Press, 1988)

Anderson, David Brown *Notes of a Rambler* (London: Houlston & Sons, 1901)

Banks, Iain *The Steep Approach to Garbadale* (London: Little, Brown Book Group, 2007)

Baxter, Peter *Perth: Past and Present* (Perth: John McKinlay, 1929)

Bell, J. J. *The Glory of Scotland* (London: George G. Harrap & Company Ltd, 1932)

Brazier, Lysbeth *The Hill o' Kinnoull* (Glasgow: James S. Kerr, 1964)

Campbell, Alexander *A Journey from Edinburgh through Parts of North Britain* (London: T.N.Longman & O. Rees, 1802)

Carr, Sir John *Caledonian Sketches or a Tour Through Scotland in 1807* (London: Mathews & Leigh, 1809)

Chambers, Robert *The Picture of Scotland* (Edinburgh: William Tait, 1828)

Connolly, Billy *Billy Connolly: The Authorized Version*, (London: Pan Books Ltd, 1976)

Courtenay, Ashley *Let's Halt Awhile* (London: Collins, 1956)

Diggle, Elizabeth *Journal of a Tour from London to the Highlands of Scotland, 19 April to 7 August 1788* (University of Glasgow Special Collections: unpublished paper notebook, 1788)

Douglas, Sheila *Fair Upon Tay: A Tayside Anthology* (Tayside Regional Council Education Department, 1992)

Drummond, Peter Robert P*erthshire in Bygone Days* (London: W. B. Whittingham & Company, 1879)

Duff, David (editor) *Queen Victoria's Highland Journals* (London: Webb & Bower, 1980)

Duncan, Jeremy *Perth and Kinross: The Big County* (Edinburgh: John Donald Publishers Ltd, 1997)

Duncan, Jeremy *Perth: A Century of Change – The Fair City 1900-2000* (Derby: The Breedon Books Publishing Company Ltd, 2008)

Dunn, Douglas (editor) *Scotland: An Anthology* (London: HarperCollins, 1991)

Durie, Alastair J. *Scotland for the Holidays – a history of tourism in Scotland, 1780-1939* (East Linton: Tuckwell Press Ltd, 2003)

Durie, Alastair J. (editor) *Travels in Scotland 1788-1881: a selection from contemporary tourist journals* (Woodbridge: Boydall Press, 2012)

Evans, Joan and John Howard Whitehouse *The Diaries of John Ruskin 1835-1847* (Oxford: Clarendon Press, 1956)

Faujas de Saint-Fond, Barthélemy *Travels in England, Scotland and The Hebrides* (London: James Ridgway, 1799)
Ferguson, Malcolm *A Tour Through The Highlands of Perthshire* (Glasgow: David Robertson, 1870)
Fairbairn, Nicholas *A Life Is Too Short* (London: Quartet Books, 1987)
Findlay, William H. *Heritage of Perth* (Perth: Photolog Press, 1984)
Finlay, Ian *The Central Highlands* (London: B. T. Batsford, 1976)
Ford, Robert *The Harp of Perthshire* (Paisley: Alexander Gardner, 1893)
Fraser, Duncan *Discovering East Scotland* (Montrose: Standard Press, 1975)

Gordon, Seton *Highways and Byways in the Central Highlands* (London: MacMillan and Company Ltd, 1948)
Graham-Campbell, David *Portrait of Perth, Angus and Fife* (London: Robert Hale Ltd, 1979)
Green, Samuel Gosnell *Scotland 100 Years Ago* (London: Bracken Books, 1985)

Hall, Andy *A Sense of Belonging to Scotland: the favourite places of Scottish personalities* (Edinburgh: Mercat Press Ltd, 2002)
Hall, Reverend James *Travels in Scotland by an Unusual Route: with a trip to the Orkneys and Outer Hebrides* (London: J. Johnson, 1807)
Harding, Bill *On Flows the Tay: Perth and the First World War* (Dunfermline: Cualann Press, 2000)
Harris, Paul *Scotland. An Anthology* (London: Cadogan Publications Ltd, 1985)
Heron, Robert *Observations made in a Journey through the Western Counties of Scotland* (Perth: R. Morrison & Sons, 1793)
Hill, Rowland *Journal of a Tour through the North of England and Parts of Scotland* (London: T. Gillett, 1799)
House, Jack *Pride of Perth* (London: Hutchinson Benham Ltd, 1976)

Jardine, Quntin *Fallen Gods* (London: Headline Book Publishing, 2003)

Lettice, John *Letters on a Tour through Various Parts of Scotland in 1792* (London: T. Cadell, 1794)
Leyden, John *Journal of a Tour in the Highlands and Western Islands of Scotland in 1800* (Edinburgh: William Blackwood & Sons, 1903)

Lindsay, Maurice *The Discovery of Scotland* (London: Robert Hale Ltd, 1964)

Macky, John *A Journey Through Scotland* (London: J. Pemberton & J. Hooke, 1723)

Martin, Peter *A Dog Called Perth* (London: Orion Books Ltd, 2001)

McCormack, David *Memories of Perth in Verse and Prose* (Perth: D. Leslie, 1956)

McGonagall, William *Poetic Gems* (London: Duckworth, 1955)

McFadden, David W. *An Innocent In Scotland* (Toronto: McLelland & Stewart Inc., 1999)

McLaren, Moray *Shell Guide to Scotland* (London: Ebury Press, 1965)

McLeish, Alexander *Songs of St Johnston* (Perth: Wood & Son, 1899)

Melville, Lawrence *The Fair Land of Gowrie* (Coupar Angus: William Culross & Son Ltd, 1939)

Miles, Hamish *Fair Perthshire* (London: John Lane The Bodley Head Ltd, 1930)

Millais, J. G. *The Life and Letters of Sir John Everett Millais* (London: Methuen & Company Ltd, 1899)

Moncrieff, A. R. Hope *The Heart of Scotland* (London: Adam & Charles Black Ltd, 1909)

Moncrieff, A. R. Hope *Scotland* (London: Adam & Charles Black Ltd, 1932)

Moncrieff, George Scott *Scottish Country* (London: Wishart Books Ltd, 1935)

Morton, James *The Dusty Road From Perth* (Vancouver: Douglas & McIntyre Ltd, 1981)

Morton, H. V. *In Search Of Scotland* (London: Methuen & Company Ltd, 1929)

Murray, The Hon. Mrs Sarah *A Companion and Useful Guide to the Beauties of Scotland* (London: George Nicol, 1799)

Murray, W. H., J. S. Grant, Seton Gordon, Tom Weir, John R. Allan, and Moray McLaren *Scotland's Splendour* (Glasgow: William Collins & Company Ltd, 1960)

Newte, Thomas *Prospects and Observations on a Tour of England and Scotland – Natural, Economical, and Literary* (London: G. G. J. & J. Robinson, 1791)

Ogilvy, Graham *The River Tay And Its People* (Edinburgh: Mainstream Publishing, 1993)

Paton, Donald N. M. *Twixt Castle and Mart* (Perth: Perth & Kinross Libraries, 2005)

Penny, George *Traditions of Perth* (Perth: Dewar. Sidey. Morison. Peat & Drummond, 1836)

Percy, W. S. *Strolling Through Scotland* (London: Collins, 1934)

Potter, Beatrix *The Journal of Beatrix Potter from 1881-1897. Transcribed from her code writing by Leslie Linder* (London: Frederick Warne & Company Ltd, 1966)

Roughead, William *Mainly Murder* (London: Cassell & Company Ltd, 1937)

Ruskin, John *Praeterita* (London: George Allen, 1899)

Roy, Kenneth *Travels In A Small Country* (Ayr: Carrick Publishing, 1987)

Roy, Kenneth *Small Country: Ten Years of the Scottish Review 1995-2004* (Glasgow: ICS Books, 2004)

Royal Association for the Promotion of the Fine Arts in Scotland *Illustrations of the Scenery of the River Tay* (Glasgow: T. & R. Annan, 1891)

Russell, Michael W. *In Waiting: Travels in the Shadow of Edwin Muir* (Glasgow: Neil Wilson Publishing, 2000)

Steven, Campbell *Enjoying Perthshire* (Perth: Perth & Kinross District Libraries, 1994)

Thomson, Arthur Alexander *Let's See The Highlands* (London: Herbert Jenkins Ltd, 1931)

Tod, Andrew (editor) *Memoirs of a Highland Lady/Elizabeth Grant of Rothiemurchus* (Edinburgh: Canongate Publishing Ltd, 1982)

Tranter, Nigel *The Queen's Scotland: The Heartland – the alphabetical, place by place guide to Stirlingshire, Perthshire and Clackmannanshire* (London: Hodder & Stoughton, 1971)

Urquhart, Alexander Reid *Auld Perth* (Perth: John Macgregor & Company, 1906)

Newspapers, Books and Magazines

Gambit – Edinburgh University Review; Perthshire Advertiser; Scotland on Sunday; Scottish Field; The Courier; The Herald;The Spectator

Web Resources

Oxford Dictionary of National Biography **www.oxforddnb.com**

Scottish Review **www.scottishreview.net**

Wilson, J., *A Perthshire Diary* **www.perthshirediary.com**

THE AUTHOR

DONALD N. M. PATON was born and educated in Perth. He has spent most of his working life in publishing and has maintained a lifetime interest in the literature, traditions, and culture of Scotland. As secretary of the Perth Burns Club for 35 years, Donald has been the instigator of popular local events such as Perth's Day of Scottish Culture now in its eleventh year. A Fellow of the Society of Antiquaries of Scotland, Donald divides his year between Perth and West Vancouver in British Columbia, Canada. This is his second book: his first, *Twixt Castle and Mart*, on Perth's historic Needless Road, was published in 2005.

THE PUBLISHER

TIPPERMUIR BOOKS LTD is a publishing company based in Perth, Scotland. It was founded in 2009 by Rob Hands and Paul Philippou. This is the company's seventh book to date. The other six are:

Spanish Thermopylae (2009)

Battleground Perthshire (2009)

Perth: Street by Street (2012)

Born in Perthshire (2012)

In Spain with Orwell (2013)

Trust (2014)

TIPPERMUIR
· BOOKS LIMITED ·